I MARRIED A PRINCESS

To GITTEL
WITH MY BEST WISHES.

Tom Scarp

25/8/12.

First published in 2009 by

WOODFIELD PUBLISHING LTD
Bognor Regis ~ West Sussex ~ England ~ PO21 5EL
www.woodfieldpublishing.com

© Thomas Soars, 2009

All rights reserved.
No part of this publication may be reproduced
or transmitted in any form or by any means,
electronic or mechanical, nor may it be stored
in any information storage and retrieval system,
without prior permission from the publisher.

The right of Thomas Soars
to be identified as Author of this work
has been asserted in accordance with
the Copyright, Designs and Patents Act 1988

ISBN 1-84683-064-8

I Married a Princess

The true story of how an English Naval Sub-Lieutenant came to marry a Persian princess during World War II

THOMAS SOARS

Woodfield

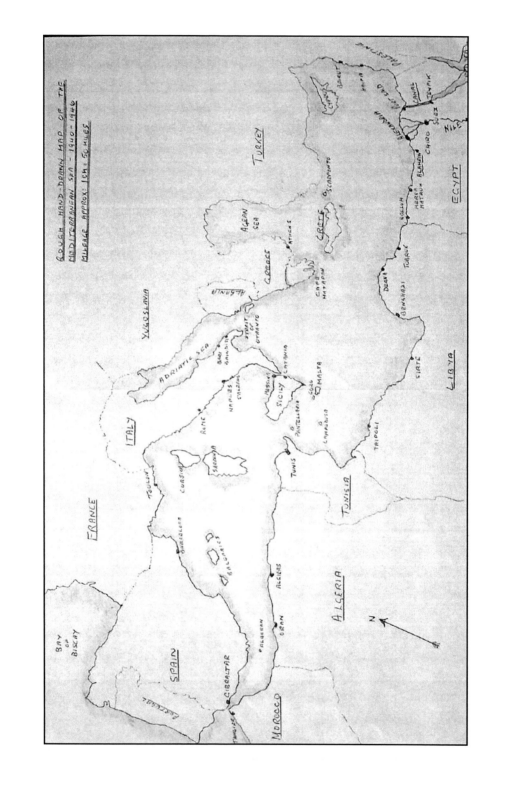

~ CONTENTS ~

Prologue .... *iii*
Acknowledgement .... *iv*
Introduction .... *v*

1. Outward Bound 1
2. Arrival in Egypt – First Impressions................. 8
3. A Cushy Number 15
4. The Tide of War Turns 23
5. To Sea Is Not To Be 29
6. Back to School 36
7. Un Coup de Foudre 41
8. Evacuation 48
9. An Unexpected Escapade 55
10. Affianced ~ and Godparents! 63
11. Back to Blighty 67
12. Prelude to *King Alfred* 73
13. Drill, Depth Charges and 'Dipping Daisy' 78
14. Back to the Med 88
15. Once Again in Alex 95
16. A Ship in the Desert 101
17. Trials and Tribulations of an O.O.D. 108
18. Requesting Permission to Marry 115
19. Surgery and a Sick Cow 133
20. A Dog Called 'Salvage' 139
21. A Child is Born 145
22. Exodus 151

23.	Oh to be in England!	161
24.	If You Know the Right People…	166
25.	Impulse Buying	170
26.	Moving In	177
27.	Easy Come, Easy Go	181
28.	Summer's Lease	185
29.	The Winter of our Discontent	188
30.	Farewell to 'Berwyn'	193
31.	A Small World	198
	Epilogue	*202*

Prologue

This is a true story about what many described at the time as an impossible romance, doomed to failure, between two young people of completely different cultures and set against a background of tensions and diversions in the Middle East, during the period of the Second World War from 1940 until 1946.

Often, it has been said that, as one ages, distant memory usually improves – often to the extent that one can even remember things that have never actually happened!

I therefore hasten to assure readers of the following pages that, in my particular case, all the incidents related *did* take place and that any temptation to exaggerate or distort has been rigorously avoided.

They say that memoirs are published for various reasons: ill-disguised vanity, a desire to relive happy bygone days, a wish to provide personal recollections of important historical happenings, and, perchance, the opportunity to make some money!

My honest nature prompts me to plead guilty to all of these reasons but, most particularly, to the last mentioned!

Acknowledgement

To my very good friends, Graham and Winifred Hughes who, when I mentioned in a letter that I had in mind writing this book, replied encouragingly:

> "Thank you for sending us copies of the first two chapters of your book which we thoroughly enjoyed reading. It is so wonderful to be able to remember one's distant past in such detail and then to be able to recount it in an interesting fashion.
>
> If your book is never published, your grandchildren will, we are sure, have great fun reading it, especially as the quality of life in those days was so different from what they expect and experience to-day."

Introduction

"How on earth did you come to marry a princess?" is a question which, if one happens to be a 'royal', would never be asked, but when one is merely a member of the lower orders – i.e. a commoner – I suppose that such an enquiry can be regarded as reasonable.

Well, let me explain… I suppose that the chain of events which led eventually to this unusual union was really set in motion on that fateful Sunday morning of September 3rd 1939, when my family and I were clustered around our radio, listening intently and with some trepidation to the sombre declaration of the Prime Minister, Neville Chamberlain, that Britain was now at war with Germany, as a result of that nation's unprovoked invasion of Poland.

The following day, King George VI addressed the population from Buckingham Palace, warning us that "the task will be hard" and that "there may be dark days ahead."

The "dark days" did not materialize immediately, instead we entered the 'phoney war' – the calm before the storm – during which Britain was given the opportunity to rebuild its Army, Navy and Air Force, all of which had been severely neglected ever since the conclusion of the First World War.

Conscription was quickly introduced and all young men who were not employed in vital industries began to be called to the colours in their age groups.

In the Insurance Company where I worked, in Brighton, Sussex, my colleagues immediately senior to me were recruited, one-by-one and, without being offered any choice, drafted into the army. I did not cherish the prospect of becoming a soldier. My father had served in the navy throughout the First World War and, having spent many hours listening to his stirring accounts of his exploits, I was most keen to join "The Senior Service".

However, it seemed that the only way I could be sure of accomplishing this was to volunteer, rather than to wait until my call-up date in March 1940.

The Branch Manager of my company was sympathetic and agreed to my resigning in January if I could be certain that the navy would accept me, so I hastily applied at the local naval recruiting office and was sent down to Portsmouth for an interview, following which I was offered a job in the Writer Branch. I was disappointed, as I had hoped to join as a Seaman, but I was told very firmly that, because of my previous clerical experience, I would be of more use to the Admiralty working in a similar capacity.

It was a case of 'Hobson's choice'.

I passed the written and medical examinations without much difficulty and was instructed to report to H.M.S. *Drake* (the naval base at Devonport) by January 30th to join the new entry training programme.

Within three days of my arrival, disaster struck! Leaving the mess-hall one evening in the strict black-out, I fell down a flight of stone steps and fractured my ankle. I was whisked off, by ambulance, to Stonehouse Naval Hospital where, after the application of a plaster cast, I was wheeled into an enormous ward containing about forty other invalids, almost all of whom, I discovered the following day, were victims of an influenza epidemic which was raging in south-west England at that time.

Three days later I also developed flu symptoms, which eventually became bronchitis, and it was not until the beginning of April that I was pronounced fit enough to return to the barracks, where I was disappointed to find that my class had almost completed the initial training.

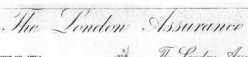

```
TELEPHONE NO. 1855/6.
TELEGRAMS: "LONCHUS," BRIGHTON.

SUB-BRANCH:
MAIDSTONE: 1. BRIDGE WHARF, HIGH STREET.

FIRE   LIFE   ACCIDENT   MARINE
```

The London Assurance House,
28-29, Richmond Place,
Brighton.

T. PYM, DISTRICT MANAGER.

20th October, 1939.
Friday.

The Commodore,
Royal Naval Barracks,
PORTSMOUTH.

Dear Sir,

    Mr. T. H. Soars of No. 54c, Coombe Road, Brighton, has applied to me for a reference in connection with his enrolment in the Royal Navy.

    During the three years which he has been at this Office, I have formed a high opinion of the manner in which his work is executed. He has shown himself to be very willing and industrious indeed, and I do not hesitate to vouch for his personal integrity.

    There is not the slightest doubt in my mind that he will fulfil in a most satisfactory manner any duties which he may be called upon to perform in his intended sphere.

Yours faithfully,

KEJ/MW   CHIEF CLERK /f/ District Manager.

The reference letter supplied by my employers to the RN.

I would have to wait until the next batch of Probationary Writers was scheduled to start training in June.

In the meantime, to keep me occupied, I was given various odd jobs in the base Pay Office and there gathered much basic information on the intricacies of naval accounting, which would be of use in future assignments.

Local leave was easy to obtain and, with another "writer-in-waiting" (who had also been sick) I was able to spend several pleasant long weekends in Exmouth, where he lived.

All such leaves were abruptly cancelled in mid-May when the news of the German blitzkrieg in Holland and Belgium came through. Once in Belgium, the enemy armoured divisions advanced around the western extremity of the much-vaunted Maginot Line and pushed rapidly through France towards the English Channel.

The miracle of Dunkirk followed, when almost four hundred thousand troops, trapped on the beaches, were rescued by a veritable armada of volunteer vessels of all types, from pleasure craft to fishing trawlers, operating under extremely hazardous conditions.

Tucked away in this remote corner of south-western England, the war seemed very distant, until one morning when an urgent message was piped through the barracks, appealing for any French-speaking personnel to report immediately to the Officer of the Day. I reported, with a handful of other ratings, to find that we were required to assist with a large influx of crews from French vessels that had managed to leave their home ports before the enemy advance made this impossible.

I was glad to have a change from the Pay Office routine and was appointed as a sort of liaison officer for a group of about forty frustrated Frenchmen! I had to ensure that they all understood the barracks routine and to help out with their victualling and accommodation arrangements.

After Maréchal Philippe Pétain surrendered in the middle of June, all the French personnel were assembled on the parade-ground, where they were addressed by their own senior officer and were given the choice of returning to France to live under the Vichy government or to remain as members of the Free French forces, headed by General de Gaulle. Many opted to return to France. These, I noticed, were the older ratings – no doubt married and concerned about the fate of their families – whilst the majority of the younger men were keen to continue the fight under de Gaulle. Several mêlées broke out as shipmates tried to prevent one another crossing the line which had been drawn on the parade-ground.

A few days after this unfortunate happening, I was finally directed to join the new class of Writers for training and, just at this time, the Luftwaffe stepped up its night-time raids on British cities – and Plymouth became one of their regular targets.

Our class had to take its turn on ARP (Air Raid Protection) duties, which involved tedious nocturnal watches on the roofs of the barrack buildings, keeping an eye out for incendiary bombs. When we were not on watch, our night's sleep would often be interrupted when the intensity of the raids would force us to take cover in one of several subterranean shelters on the base. Considerable damage to buildings was caused by high-explosive bombs, but there were surprisingly few casualties.

By the end of August, we sat for our final examinations and, after a few days, received the news that the entire class had passed, whereupon we celebrated in style at the famous Goodbody's restaurant in the city.

The following morning we were happy to learn that we would be allowed seven days home leave prior to being drafted for service overseas – the "buzz" prevalent in the base being that, in all probability, this could mean the Middle East.

I travelled home to Brighton where, in the company of family and friends, the week passed all too quickly but even there – a seaside resort of no strategic value – we received, on two occasions, the unwelcome attentions of the Luftwaffe as their bombers, having been chased away from their main objective, London, jettisoned their lethal loads on the coast, prior to escaping back across the Channel.

I also took the opportunity to pay a farewell visit to the office of my old employers and, whilst there, it suddenly occurred to me that it might be useful to have the names and addresses of the Company's representatives in the Levant area.

As I carefully folded the list and tucked it away in my wallet, little did I know that this piece of paper was to be the instrument to lead me eventually to a young woman of royal descent who would consent to become my life partner…

1. Outward Bound

It was a momentous journey back to Devonport after my leave. I boarded an evening train from Brighton, which made good time until it reached the outskirts of London, where it shuddered to a sudden halt. Word came through that a heavy air-raid was in progress in the city and it was some time before the train resumed its journey towards its destination.

Never will I forget the awesome vista down-river towards the East End as, cautiously, the train ventured across Victoria Bridge. On both banks of the Thames, blazing buildings were reflected in the water, and the acrid smell of smoke filtered into the railway carriage.

Descending to the Underground, on arrival, to obtain my connection at Paddington Station, I was confronted with the sad spectacle of platforms covered with families preparing to settle down for a safe night's sleep and, when my train arrived, I had to tread carefully over several recumbent persons in order to board it.

I found Paddington crowded with returning servicemen and refugee families, mostly women and children laden with baggage, all eager to get away from the violence in London and to reach the comparative safety of the West Country.

It was a long, sleepless night, for the train made several stoppages en route and did not arrive at the North Road Station in Plymouth until after 9am.

I reported to the Drafting Office on entering the barracks and, immediately, I was placed on the pre-embarkation routine, consisting of medical and dental examinations and an unpleasant range of inoculations.

Four feverish days later, I joined a whole trainload of naval personnel bound for an unknown destination and, after a long and tedious journey, the train finished up at Glasgow at around noon the following day. There, at the station, awaited a fleet of charabancs, which transported us to the dockland area, where we embarked on the White Star cruise ship *Georgic,* which, once loaded, proceeded slowly down the Firth of Clyde to Gourock, where we joined up with a convoy of several other large vessels.

An amusing incident occurred as we were all crowded on deck, taking in the beauty of the Scottish countryside which many of us realized we would not be seeing again for possibly many years. A golf course gradually came into view on the ship's starboard side and, very close to the water's edge, we saw a tee, with a foursome preparing to make their drives. One golfer was just about to take a swing at his ball when he was subjected to a chorus of ribald epithets from the seamen leaning over the rails. Visibly shaken, he missed the ball completely, and subsequently, to give vent to his feelings, turned in our direction and, with a mighty wallop, drove the ball clean over our heads, to land with a loud clang against one of the ship's funnels, whereupon he was given a hearty, good-natured cheer from all on board.

The *Georgic* had been only partially refitted as a troopship and on one deck there were still many cabins in their pre-war state. I was fortunate enough to be allocated to one of these, along with two other Writers, who had been on the new entry course with me.

That night we all slept like logs and awakened the following morning to discover that we were out of sight of land and the ship pitching and tossing through heavy seas. *Mal de mer* soon claimed many of us and the mess halls were almost empty.

It took about 24 hours for my two cabin-mates and myself to recover and gain our sea-legs. Emerging weakly on deck, we were astonished to find a large bevy of khaki-clad women. Only then did we become aware that we had on board the first contingent of A.T.S. to be destined for Middle East duties. Apparently, they had all been sick since leaving port, and after we comforted one poor soul who was still having trouble keeping her breakfast down, she gazed up wanly at us and said, "I do so envy you sailors never having to suffer like this."

We "sailors" accepted her approbation – without letting on that this was our first time at sea!

Later that day, alarm bells sounded and we donned our lifejackets, as instructed, and proceeded on deck to find that the convoy was under aerial attack. Two German Junkers were circling the convoy amidst a violent anti-aircraft barrage from our escort vessels and, now fascinated, we watched the planes fly over the troopships on the far side of the convoy from us , dropping their bomb-loads.

Several enormous plumes of water erupted but then, suddenly, one of the bombs found its mark and a flash of fire and smoke appeared on the after deck of one of the vessels.

Finally, to our relief, the attackers were driven off and we later learned that the damaged troopship had been ordered to return to port, escorted by one of the destroyers.

Ever since leaving Devonport we had been under the impression that we were destined for the Middle East, via the Cape of Good Hope, but we began to have doubts, as the convoy's course continued in a westerly direction, as though we were bound for North America. On the third day our doubts were put to rest when the course abruptly changed to south-east and, gradually, the weather became warmer as we approached the coast of West Africa.

One morning we awakened to find that we had slackened speed and, shortly afterwards, we heard the ship's anchor chains being run out.

Our landfall was Freetown, the capital of Sierra Leone, and rushing up on deck we found that it was akin to entering a sauna bath as we encountered the full blast of a hot, humid, offshore wind.

An announcement was made that there would be no shore leave, as the medical authorities ashore advised against this, due to a recent epidemic of some kind of tropical disease. However, this did not prevent an armada of primitive native boats (actually hollowed-out tree trunks) paddling out from shore and surrounding the various ships in the harbour.

These craft were laden stem to stern with local produce such as bananas, coconuts, mangoes and other species of fruit which we did not recognise. Trading was soon in full swing as baskets of produce were hoisted up from the boats to the *Georgic* passengers in exchange for articles of clothing which, curiously, the natives insisted on in preference to money.

There was no black-out in force that night and it was a very pleasant change for us to be able to see the illuminated buildings ashore, as well as the lights on all the vessels in the harbour.

Due to the extreme heat, sleep did not come easily and it was a relief the following morning when the convoy left the harbour, when, once under way, we were able to enjoy the cooling sea breezes.

Proceeding south, we soon reached the equator, where a day-long boisterous "crossing the line" ceremony was held, but in the midst of all the high jinks we were suddenly reminded that we were still navigating in potentially dangerous waters when our escort cruiser came quite close and we watched whilst her Walrus seaplane took off to carry out dive-bombing manoeuvres. (Although, by this time, the menace of German pocket battleship surface raiders had been eliminated, several reports had been received that there were still U-boats prowling around in these waters.)

Soon the weather began to turn cooler and, just prior to our arrival at the Cape on 28th October, the order came for us to switch from tropical whites to our blues.

At Simonstown we were welcomed by a huge crowd of local citizens and as soon as shore leave was announced, JC (a fellow Writer) and I were quickly down the gangway to the quayside where, in no time, we were offered a lift to the town centre, about eighteen miles distant.

Once there, I made enquiries about the location of the Cape Town branch of the Insurance Company I had worked for in England and, despite arriving at the office without prior warning, we were overwhelmed by a most cordial reception by the Manager and his staff. Later, over lunch, he explained that I happened to be the first member of the UK staff in uniform to visit his office.

Returning to the office, the amount of work done that afternoon must have been negligible for the excited female employees abandoned their typewriters to busy themselves organising a garden party to take place at the home of one of the girls, who lived in an attractive suburb on the outskirts of the city.

We danced and made merry until almost midnight, by which time we had to leave to be back on board before one o'clock in the morning.

After completing various chores the following morning, we were again allowed shore leave, commencing at mid-day, and, in accordance with tentative arrangements we had made the previous day, we were taken on a sight-seeing tour by two of the girls, who had taken a half-day off from the office for what they considered was a special occasion!

That evening we were invited to another party, this time a barbecue on one of the beautiful beaches nearby.

On the return trip to the ship we made plans for the following day but, alas, it was not to be… We were awakened early to the disconcerting sound of gangways being lowered and, by mid-morning, the entire convoy crept out of the harbour.

It was with heavy hearts that we stood on deck, watching Cape Agulhas, the most southerly point on the African continent, slowly recede into the distance as we headed north into the Indian Ocean.

There had been no way of getting the news of our pending departure to our new-found friends who would only have become aware of our leaving when they made. the long drive down to the docks.

Before going below, my friend JC turned to me and said "Maybe we should have skipped ship and stayed there."

Miserably, I nodded my head in agreement.

We were not altogether surprised when we heard the following day that several fellows had indeed done that! I often wonder how they fared.

Durban and Mombasa had both been spoken about as possible future ports of call but we did not stop again until after we rounded the Horn of Africa and, on a viciously hot afternoon, entered the harbour at Aden, where we joined up with another convoy.

We left Aden the following day and passed through the narrow sea passage – only about ten miles wide – which at that point separates Asia from Africa and entered the Red Sea. We were now sailing northwards on the last lap of our marathon voyage with, on the port side, the distant outline of the Eritrean coast and, to starboard, the yellow Sinai desert stretching as far as the eye could see.

During the last few days I had taken advantage of an offer made by an RAF officer (who had previously spent some years in Egypt) to give Arabic lessons to anyone who was interested and I had found the language complicated but very fascinating. The basic words and phrases which I learned would prove to be of considerable value in the years ahead.

I was thankful for the diversion these classes provided, for the daily routine on board was becoming more and more monotonous and was broken only by two unusual incidents – one when someone fell overboard, but was fortunate enough to be spotted and picked up by the last ship in line, and the other when our escorting destroyer came alongside to take off two nursing sisters in order to transport them to another vessel, where, apparently, someone had been taken dangerously ill.

Finally, we left the Red Sea and, entering the Gulf of Suez, we berthed at what was to be our final destination, Port Tewfik, at the southern end of the Canal, through which, in more peaceful times, our ship would have sailed to the Mediterranean.

On 17th November the naval contingent disembarked at an ungodly hour and, lugging our kitbags and hammocks, swarmed aboard an ancient train for the journey 100 miles north to Port Said.

As I sat back in the uncomfortable, crowded, sand-covered, windowless carriage, I reflected on the six-week voyage I had just undertaken – a total of approximately 15 thousand miles. Quite an epic journey for one whose longest sea trip hitherto had been from Newhaven to Boulogne and back on a school outing!

2. Arrival in Egypt – First Impressions

As a result of several lengthy halts en route, our train did not pull into Port Said station until the early afternoon. Despite the heat and physical discomfort, I had found the journey along the western bank of the Suez Canal most interesting. As we passed mile after mile of this strategic waterway I could not help being filled with admiration for the genius and determination of its creator, Ferdinand de Lesseps, who, almost one hundred years ago had persuaded the French, British and Egyptian governments to finance this colossal undertaking to join the Mediterranean to the Red Sea.

We had seen many sites of historical significance en route, including a magnificent granite monument standing on high ground, which, we were informed, commemorated the allied forces' defence of the Canal during World War I against repeated attacks by German-supported Turkish armies.

After alighting from the train, our large naval contingent was lined up on the platform in readiness for inspection by a harassed-looking RNVR Lieutenant, assisted by a Petty Officer.

They walked down the lines, checking on the draft chits held by the different categories of ratings, before directing them to the awaiting lorries. When they arrived at our group of sixteen Writer and Supply Branch ratings, all of whom held papers indicating that we were being 'sent to HMS *Nile* for disposal', we were surprised to be told by the officer, "You shouldn't be here".

Apparently, HMS *Nile* was the naval shore base in Alexandria and someone in authority should have made sure that we had changed trains at Ismaila – a city I recollected passing through about fifty miles south of Port Said.

There are few situations in life more depressing than to arrive at a destination after a long and wearisome journey only to told that you are at the wrong place! No southbound train for the return trip being available until the following day, we were ordered into one of the lorries, along with the other ratings, and then the entire convoy set off towards the harbour, where Navy House was located. There, thankfully, a meal was provided, after which we were told that, as the accommodation was filled to overflowing, we would be spending the night on the *Cairo City*.

This turned out to be an antique, rusting vessel moored in the harbour and being used by the naval base for temporary accommodation. On arriving on board, we were pleased to be informed that it would not be necessary to use our hammocks, as cots, with mattresses, were available below deck. Our joy at this unanticipated luxury was soon to be dispelled, however, for within a short time of turning in, we all began fidgeting and scratching as we discovered that the mattresses were heavily bug-infested. We had no choice but to abandon the cots and sling our hammocks up on deck where, exhausted from the day's travelling, all of us were soon lulled to sleep under a starlit sky.

We were awakened at around 5.30am by the noisy duty Petty Officer and, without having time for a wash, were hurried back to the Navy House for a very brief breakfast before being transported back to the railway station. There we boarded the train for yet another bone-rattling itinerary – this time, hopefully, to our proper destination, Alexandria, about two hundred miles distant.

We made sure that we changed trains at Ismailia where, after a brief wait, we boarded the west-bound train for Alexandria. The crowded train made very slow progress as it meandered its way through a flat agricultural landscape, stopping at several small towns, of similar appearance – a cluster of flat-topped houses surrounding mosques with lofty, slender minarets. At every station, hordes of clamorous native vendors invaded the carriages, eager to sell their wares of every description.

The Arabic lessons I had taken aboard the *Georgic* now came in handy and, in record time, I picked up the shopping routine. No prices appeared on the natives' goods; one simply pointed to the item in which you were interested and asked *"bi kam da?"* (how much?). The answer could be, say, twenty piastres, whereupon one would frown and say *"da ghali"* (that's expensive), whereupon, with much wailing and calling on Allah for assistance, the price would be lowered. Again you would repeat *"da ghali"* and eventually, after much haggling, you would obtain the desired article for, say, five piastres – the amount of its true value!

At around midday we reached Benha – the main junction on the Alexandria to Cairo main line – where, to our annoyance, we were politely informed by the station-master that we had missed our connection and thus had almost a two-hour wait for the north-bound Alex train. With time on our hands, most of us were eager to venture into the town but, having been warned before leaving Port Said to keep a careful watch on our belongings, it was agreed that we would split into two parties so that the kitbags and hammocks, now piled high on the dusty platform, could be guarded at all times.

Leaving the precincts of the station with the first group, I was quite unprepared for the scene which awaited us. For a person fresh from England, it was literally overwhelming. As we wandered through the maze of narrow streets, which were strewn with reeking refuse of all kinds, a mixture of odours assailed our nostrils, ranging from manure to burning charcoal, to various smells of food being cooked. Soon we were followed by a motley crowd of begging youngsters, clad in rags, who kept up an incessant chorus of *"baksheesh!"* This was just part of a veritable cacophony of noise which filled the air – dogs barking, donkeys braying in complaint at their excessive loads, merchants advertising their wares and radios blaring from inside cafés.

We passed by stalls laden with all manner of fruit and vegetables; booths displaying cages crammed with scrawny, cackling chickens, each awaiting its turn to be weighed, sold and killed; and other stalls exhibiting large slabs of meat of unknown origin, covered with swarms of flies which, from time to time, the vendors would disperse with a nonchalant wave of a fan.

We continued our way through this labyrinth of narrow lanes and, turning a corner, suddenly came face to face with a disturbing display of local justice being administered. A hefty *shawish* (police constable), brandishing a long, thin cane, was giving a full-blooded lashing to a howling young boy who was grovelling in the dust. Apparently, he had been found stealing from one of the stalls. Our first reaction was to try to intervene but we had the good sense to realize that had we done so it would, undoubtedly, have led to serious consequences for our small group. Reluctantly, with the boy's cries receding into the distance, we retraced our steps to the station, there to take our turn in guarding the luggage until the train from Cairo arrived.

By the time we finally reached Alexandria it was late in the evening but, much to our relief, there was a naval transport waiting to take us to the harbour of Ras-el-Tin where HMS *Nile* was located. Being close to midnight, no meal was available but a compassionate Duty Officer was able to muster mugs of steaming hot cocoa and biscuits for us before allocating us space in a seamen's mess, where we could sling our hammocks for the night. Dog-tired, I fell asleep almost immediately.

After a breakfast (the most appetising meal we had tasted since disembarking from the *Georgic* two days previously), six of the Writer ratings (including myself) were advised that we were to be employed in the B.A.O. (Base Accounts Office) and that transportation was being arranged to take us to "the Syracuse".

As we boarded the lorry we asked the Able Seaman Driver, "What is the Syracuse?" He informed us that it was a hotel in the centre of the city, leased by the Admiralty for overflow accommodation. The word 'overflow' immediately evoked an image of our recent unpleasant experience aboard the *Cairo City* and I was somewhat fearful of what could be in store for us!

The drive into the city took us along a magnificent seafront (known locally as 'The Corniche'), which was lined, on the landward side, with modern European-style hotels, office buildings and blocks of apartments, all facing northwards across the palm-tree-lined boulevard, with the blue Mediterranean beyond.

Alexandria's famous Corniche promenade in the 1940s.

Eventually, our driver slowed and turned down a short side-street, lined on one side with several horse-drawn *gharries* (taxis) awaiting fares, until we came to a busy thoroughfare that ran parallel to the Corniche. We then stopped on the corner, outside an imposing six-storey building, over the entrance to which was displayed the name "Hotel Syracuse".

Jumping out of the back of the lorry, we started to unload our baggage when, out of the hotel, appeared three native porters, who quickly went to work, lugging everything into the hotel lobby.

We followed them inside where, to greet us, was the hotel manager and an attractive lady whom he introduced as his wife. They welcomed us as though we were VIPs, despite the fact that we were a most rough-looking, unkempt group after our two days of travel.

A card from the Hotel Syracuse, Alexandria, Egypt in the 1940s.

After entering our names into the hotel register, the six of us were ushered into an elevator and taken to the third floor, where our rooms were located. The room to which J – a fellow Writer – and I were assigned was most impressive. It was well furnished, with twin beds, an enormous wardrobe, a balcony overlooking the side-street and, to our delight, an adjoining bathroom with, we quickly discovered, plenty of hot water in the taps!

We lost no time in showering, shaving and changing into clean shifts – all the time commenting on our good fortune in having been provided with accommodation of such unexpected comfort.

Already, the night so recently spent on the *Cairo City* was becoming just a dim memory!

3. A Cushy Number

It soon became apparent that, against all the odds, the other five ratings and I had landed in a *sinecure* or, in naval parlance, *a cushy number*. During my initial training period in Devonport Barracks I had gathered from banter picked up from knowledgeable regular servicemen that such jobs did exist, but I never dreamed that I would be fortunate enough to land one – especially in wartime!

Our place of employment, the Base Accounts Office, was housed on two floors in a fairly modern commercial building located in a suburb called Mazarita, quite close to the city centre and within easy walking distance of our "barracks" – the Hotel Syracuse. Somewhat incongruously, both locations were regarded as integral parts of HMS Nile.

Before being allocated our duties, on the morning following our arrival "on board" we were escorted by the senior Chief Writer into the hallowed presence of 'the boss' – a Paymaster Captain of advanced years, who, during his brief welcoming speech, reminded us very forcibly that we should not allow ourselves to be beguiled by the civilian trappings and to bear in mind at all times that we were still subject to all aspects of naval discipline.

When he asked if we had any questions, an intrepid member of our sextet spoke up and asked if there was any chance of his being drafted to a sea-going ship. This enquiry evoked a sharp negative response from the Captain and a frown from the Chief Writer. I got the impression that they preferred not to be reminded that they both had cushy numbers!

I quickly settled into the new routine and was given a ledger section to manage the pay accounts of the crews of several locally-based small craft. My immediate superior was an easy-going Petty Officer, an Irishman, who, very painstakingly, explained all the requirements of the work.

The office hours were very similar to those of my pre-war job, except that every five days we would be on an all-night duty watch, which necessitated sleeping on camp-beds in the office and being on the alert for any eventualities, which included the possibility of an enemy air-raid.

Shortly after my arrival we experienced one or two Italian air-raids – one bomb landing fairly close to our hotel – but we did not hear if any vital targets had suffered damage. We got the impression that the Italian pilots preferred to unload their bombs whilst flying at high level, escaping as rapidly as possible!

It was common knowledge that in June that year their planes had mistakenly bombed their own vessels instead of units of the British fleet. Happily for the Italian naval crews, their airmen's bombing was so inaccurate that no ship was hit!

Apart from these occasional alerts, Alexandrian daily life, generally speaking, continued unruffled and, for us newcomers, there was, in our off-duty hours, much to be explored in this ancient seaport founded by Alexander the Great some three hundred years B.C.

In addition to delving into the mysteries of the past by visiting museums and historical sites, we also had sufficient leisure time in which to savour present day attractions. There were excellent restaurants and cinemas showing surprisingly modern films. Also a variety of night-clubs, but the wherewithal needed to patronize these was well beyond the financial capacity of a lowly naval rating which, in retrospect, was to our benefit, for instead we turned to more healthful pursuits in our off-duty hours.

We discovered that we were able to hire bicycles very cheaply and by this means we soon became acquainted with the city and its environs and, at the same time, obtained the exercise necessary to compensate for the long office hours sitting and poring over pay ledgers.

One Sunday in mid-December, a group of us undertook a twenty-mile ride into the countryside east of the city in order to visit Aboukir Bay, the site of the famous sea battle that took place at the end of the 18th Century, when Admiral Nelson annihilated Napoleon's fleet without losing a single ship.

The day following this excursion, I developed a splitting headache, with a high temperature and a throbbing pain behind the eyes. At first, I surmised that I must be suffering from sun-stroke and, despite bouts of vomiting, I somehow managed to stagger on until the following morning, when extreme weakness forced me to report sick. By this time my condition had deteriorated so much that I was transported by ambulance to the British Forces General Hospital, located on the outskirts of the city.

There, I was diagnosed as having *sandfly fever*, a fairly common disease occurring in the countries of the eastern Mediterranean, which is transmitted by the bite of a fly called a *phlebotomus*. By this time, my temperature had soared to the point that I was feeling delirious and I was only vaguely aware of being trundled into an immense room, lined with many beds, and then losing consciousness.

It must have been some time later that I awakened to the rustling of paper and, opening my eyes, discovered the source of this. Sitting on the side of the bed next to mine was a khaki-clad figure, fiddling with a pile of multi-coloured paper strips and a pot of glue. Catching my eye, the figure, speaking with a strong Australian accent, said, "Had a good kip, mate?"

I nodded my head and enquired what he was doing.

"Those nurses mate, have got me and my cobbers making paper chains for Christmas decorations."

"What date are we?" I asked.

"December twentieth," he replied.

Miserably, I reflected that here I was, a hospital patient, only one month after my arrival in Alexandria, and I wondered whether I would be sufficiently recovered in time to rejoin my colleagues for the festive parties we had been planning.

My reveries were interrupted by the arrival of an attractive nursing sister, brandishing a thermometer, which she shoved into my mouth whilst, at the same time, checking my blood pressure.

Removing the thermometer, she scrutinized it, frowned, and shook her head, saying, "You'll have to remain in bed until we can reduce that temperature." Turning to the mobile table alongside her, she selected a handful of tablets and ordered me to swallow them with a glass of water.

Two days slowly passed before the medical officer in charge of the ward allowed me to be removed from the "strictly bed patient" list and to resume a normal diet instead of the beef tea and lemonade to which I had been restricted since being admitted.

As my condition improved, I began to take an interest in my surroundings. The ward, which was known as Ward C1 East, contained about thirty beds, occupied mostly by Australian and New Zealand troops, with just a few naval types. During conversations I discovered that, with only one or two exceptions, my fellow patients were all war casualties resulting from the ongoing allied army offensive in the Western Desert. This drive, under the command of General Wavell, had been launched in the first week of December and had already been very successful in forcing the large Italian army, which had been poised on the border between Egypt and Libya, to retreat towards the west.

On seeing the frightful wounds sustained by some of these patients, I could not help feeling that, being on the same ward as them, I was there under false pretences! As soon as I was declared to be convalescent I volunteered to assist in doing various chores in the ward, which included the preparation of Christmas decorations, but the hopes that I had been entertaining of being discharged before the twenty-fifth were dashed when, suddenly, I suffered a relapse – once again with a high temperature – and was ordered back to bed.

Fortunately, by the time Christmas arrived, I was sufficiently recovered to participate in a splendid dinner which, somehow or other, the staff had managed to conjure up for us. In addition, every patient received a stocking containing such items as soap, cigarettes, chocolate and, most surprising of all, to accompany our meal, we all were given bottles of Guinness. A unique greetings card, depicting a Santa Claus riding a camel, was given to each patient. I took mine around the ward and, to serve as a souvenir, obtained the signatures of all of my fellow patients and also those of the doctors and nurses. To this day I have this treasured memento amongst my keepsakes.

On Boxing Day a boisterous contingent from the staff of the Base Accounts Office made a surprise visit bringing letters from home and gifts of assorted delicacies. More important than the gifts was the assurance that they were able to bring me that my job was still open. I had become somewhat fearful that, because of the very short time of my employment plus the knowledge that the office was extremely busy, a replacement Writer may have been recruited.

A souvenir Xmas card, bearing signatures of the patients, doctors and nurses at the military hospital, Alexandria, Egypt, 1940.

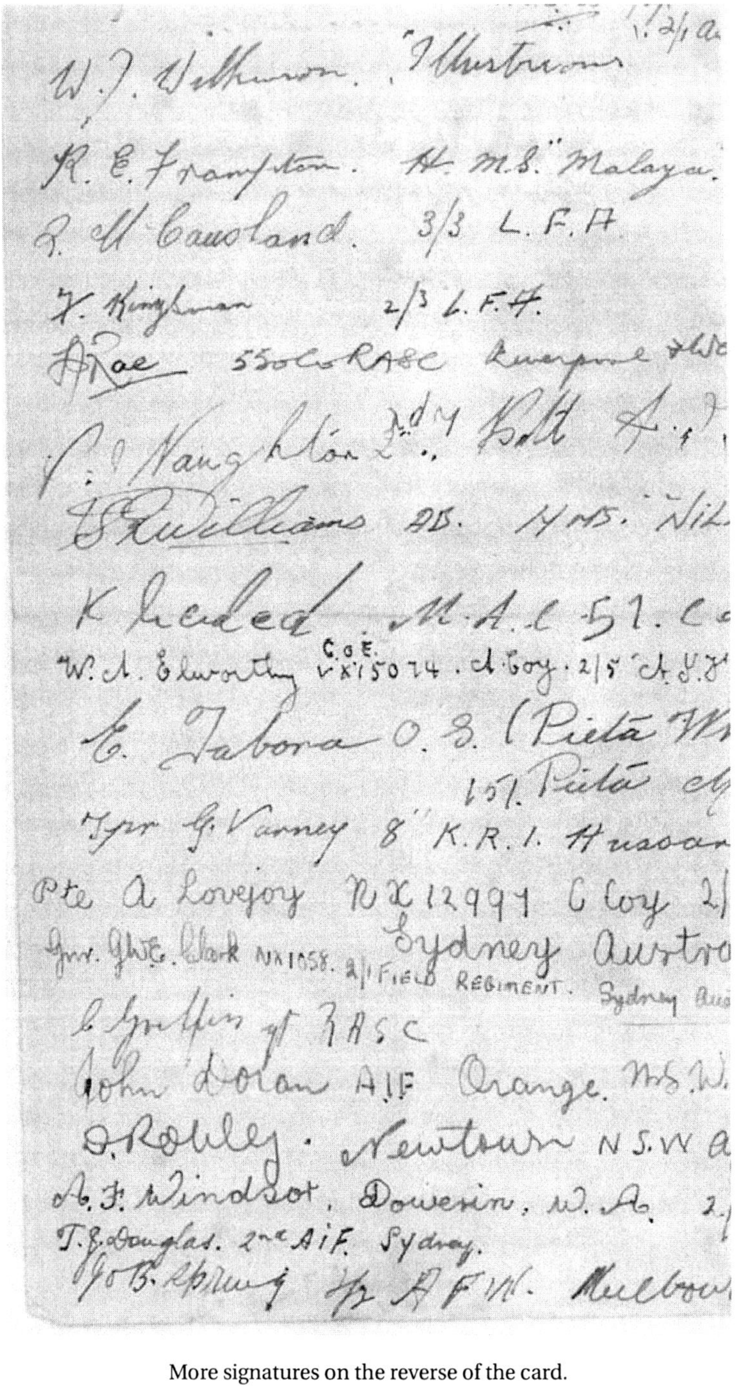

More signatures on the reverse of the card.

This visit soon developed into a hilarious party, much to the dismay of the duty nurse who finally waded in with great courage and sent all the visitors packing!

The following morning I was checked over by the M.O. and pronounced to be fit for discharge. I have no doubt that the previous day's merrymaking accelerated my release!

4. The Tide of War Turns

Arriving back at the Base Accounts Office, I was treated like a long-lost relative, especially by those of my colleagues who, in my absence, had been working on my section to keep my ledgers up-to-date.

A few days following my return, I decided that it was time to get into touch with the company which, according to the list obtained during my farewell visit to my pre-war employers, was the agency representing their interests in Egypt. The Managing Director of the company was a Swiss citizen – a Mr Paul R – a very fine gentleman in his early forties, who gave me an extremely cordial reception and informed me that I was the first member of the company's United Kingdom staff to visit his office since the outbreak of war.

Inviting me to lunch at the elegant Pastroudi's restaurant on Rue Fouad, he was keen to learn all about the wartime situation in England, where he had studied in his younger days. Also, he elaborated on his business dealings, of which, I was surprised to learn, the insurance underwriting aspect was relatively minor. His firm's main commercial interest was in the cotton business and I gathered that, for many years, they had been one of the most important exporters of this valuable commodity, much of which had finished up, before the war, in England's Lancashire cotton mills.

This meeting was to be the beginning of an amicable relationship which was to endure almost fifty years.

This friendship, during my time in Alexandria, was to prove most valuable as, in addition to meeting his charming wife and their three small children, I also became acquainted with his business partner, Mr Leonard B, and his family, as well as various members of his staff, several of whom were in my own age group. Thanks to them, I was able to enjoy the many amenities of the local Swiss Club.

In my off-duty weekends I became a regular visitor to Paul's home, which was located in an exclusive eastern residential suburb of the city and he and his wife Lilli, also extended their hospitality to any of my office colleagues whom I wished to bring along.

In short, as time passed, their home became my home and I have recollections of many happy hours spent there. When relaxing in their beautiful garden or playing a game of croquet on the lawn with their three energetic youngsters, it was difficult to imagine that war, with all its horrors, was being waged on land, sea and air only three hundred miles west of this oasis of tranquillity.

By the beginning of March 1941, the successful advance of the allied army along the Western Desert coast as far as Sirte, in Libya, had come to a halt as, following urgent appeals from the Greek Government for assistance against a German invasion, a substantial part of the allied army had to be diverted to help the Greek troops to defend their country.

Following the humiliating defeats of their Italian allies both in the Western Desert and on the Greece/Albania border, the German High Command had decided it was necessary to come to their rescue on both fronts.

As a direct result of the depletion of the Allied army in the desert, it was forced to retreat before the advance of the very highly mechanised and well-equipped Afrika Korps, under the command of General Erwin Rommel, so that, by the end of March, the strategic ports of Benghazi, Derna and Bardia had all been given up, leaving only Tobruk holding out against the enemy onslaught.

To add to these depressing reverses, we were astounded to hear over the radio one morning that, on March 24th, the backbone of Britain's naval defences, the battleship HMS *Hood*, had been sunk (with almost its entire crew) by the German battleship *Bismarck* during a brief engagement in the Denmark Strait between Greenland and Iceland.

This most bitter blow to British naval prestige was, to some extent, avenged when, after a three-day chase in the North Atlantic, the fleet caught and sank the *Bismarck* before it could reach safe shelter in one of the German-occupied French ports.

Also, at this time, the news filtered through that, in an encounter off Cape Matapan, on the southern-most coast of Greece, our Eastern Mediterranean Fleet had destroyed three Italian cruisers and two destroyers, without incurring any losses. This victory provided a much-needed boost to the morale, not only of the navy but for all elements of the Allied armed forces in the Middle East.

Unfortunately, the jubilation following this victory was destined to be short-lived, for the tide was turning against the Allies in Greece where, by the end of April, the German land forces, aided by the overwhelming air superiority of the Luftwaffe, had forced the Greek government to surrender, leaving the surviving Allied troops to withdraw to the southern part of the country, where they could be evacuated and transferred to the strategic island of Crete, which was about one hundred and fifty miles distant.

Every available naval vessel in the Eastern Med was called upon to participate in the task of evacuation, which was a hazardous operation due to the continual enemy low-level bombing attacks by planes flying from newly-established airfields, both in Greece and on the Dodecanese islands, one of which, Scarpanto, was only fifty miles away. Several of our ships were lost or damaged during this exodus but, nevertheless, over fifty thousand troops were safely withdrawn, together with much valuable equipment.

There was a temporary lull whilst the enemy consolidated its gains in Greece but, towards the end of May, a devastating full-scale attack was launched on Crete, with sustained bombing of the airfields and installations there. This was followed up by wave after wave of airborne troops being parachuted in, around the clock.

Within a week it became obvious to the Allied Command that the island, despite a most gallant resistance, could not be held much longer so, once again, a total withdrawal was ordered.

The exhausted crews of the allied ships were again called upon for assistance and, during the last days of May, thousands of retreating troops were picked up from the beaches of Crete and ferried to the safety of Alexandria, but not without appalling losses of vessels sunk or damaged by the incessant Luftwaffe dive-bombing. The final dreadful tally was three cruisers and six destroyers sunk and one aircraft carrier, three battleships, six cruisers and seven destroyers seriously damaged.

Whilst the allied casualties were high, it was estimated that their stubborn rearguard action had cost the Germans the loss of more than 400 planes and approximately 15,000 troops, of which a third were men of their crack airborne division. In retrospect, it is probably fair to say that the defence of Crete actually saved the vital island of Malta, for, following their Cretan experience, the Germans had no appetite to tackle another similar airborne operation.

During these critical days, the B.A.O. operated an emergency office at 46 Shed in the harbour. It was manned by a Paymaster Lieutenant and myself and we worked around the clock, taking care of the immediate financial and accommodation needs of groups of survivors as they were brought ashore. Many of these men had harrowing tales to tell of their experiences and, from their haggard appearances, it was plain to see that they had been to hell and back.

I spoke with some lads from the destroyer *Kelly*, who had taken to the water when their ship sank only to be strafed by machine-gun fire from low-flying enemy aircraft before the survivors could be rescued by a sister ship, the *Kipling*.

The commanding officer of *Kelly*, Captain Lord Louis Mountbatten (later to become the last Viceroy of India), clad in ill-fitting replacement clothing just acquired from the nearby naval supply store, was there, shepherding the remnants of his crew and encouraging them to put on a brave face despite their recent traumatic ordeal.

Outside, on the dockyard quays, it was a hive of activity as ambulances were continually arriving to pick up wounded survivors as they were carried down the gangways of the rescuing ships. Apart from naval personnel there were hundreds of troops, including a large number of Australian and New Zealand soldiers.

The post-Crete situation was not a happy one. Whilst the allies had been vainly attempting to save Greece and Crete, disaster was looming in the desert west of Alexandria, where Rommel was now advancing rapidly towards Egypt. Fortunately, by mid-June, the stubborn resistance of the allied army, coupled with a weakening in the long German supply line, brought the advance to a standstill near Sollum – a port just inside the Egyptian frontier. There, a stalemate set in, neither side having sufficient strength to mount a full-scale offensive.

The proximity of the enemy, now less than three hundred miles from the outskirts of Alexandria, brought to its citizens an increased awareness of the dangers they could be facing. Nocturnal air-raids now became more frequent, some involving many casualties and considerable property damage, especially in those areas close to the harbour and docks.

After one such raid, we were notified by the local police that the body of a naval officer was found amongst others in the shattered remains of a *maison de tolerance* located in a high-class neighbourhood of the city.

It so happened that his pay account was borne on the ledger of one of the vessels for which I was responsible and, when closing up the account to the date of death, it was also necessary to show the cause of death.

After a brief discussion with a sympathetic senior officer I was ordered to record it as "killed in action."

If, indeed, the poor fellow's end had come whilst he was actively occupied then, I reflected, this was, most surely, among the more pleasant of ways in which to exit this world!

5. To Sea Is Not To Be

During the critical weeks following the Crete evacuation, I had been in contact frequently with members of the crews of those destroyers whose pay ledgers I maintained and had thus been able to hear first-hand accounts of the trials and tribulations they had undergone.

I found that these encounters were beginning to stir within me something akin to a guilt feeling when I compared their hardships with the relatively comfortable way of life I was currently enjoying. True, the pressure of work in the B.A.O. had become extremely onerous, necessitating considerable overtime, and, in addition, all-night duty air raid watches had now become routine. Nevertheless, I could not divest myself of this sense of lack of fulfilment in that, last year, I had joined the navy but not by any strength of imagination could I feel that I was actually in the navy and doing my fair share of the war effort.

So, early in July, after much soul-searching, I made my intentions to seek sea service known to the Chief Writer of my Pay Section. He greeted my request with incredulity, suggesting that I "needed my head examined" but, seeing that my mind was made up, he agreed, reluctantly, to pass on my request to our Paymaster Lieutenant for attention.

A day or two later I was summoned to the Paymaster's office. I was somewhat surprised to receive quite a sympathetic hearing from this officer, who admitted that he could well understand my feelings and that he, himself, was of like mind. However, he made it quite clear that, at this stage, he could not recommend that my request be directed further "up the ladder", in view of the fact that the office was severely understaffed and extra hands were needed to cope with the ever-increasing work volume. However, he confided in me that within a few months this situation could well change as, quite recently, signals had been received from the C-in-C's office to the effect that a large contingent of Wrens was to be sent out from England with a view to their taking over many of the shore duties in the various naval establishments in Alexandria and Port Said, thus making available the male incumbents for sea-going service.

"But, who knows," he said, with a twinkle in his eye, as I was leaving his office. "When all those young women land here, you may have second thoughts about going to sea!"

As I returned to my desk, I was turning over in my mind why the Admiralty should even be considering sending a crowd of young women into an active war zone, the front line of which was just one day's drive west of Alexandria.

After this setback I had no choice but to resign myself to a summer of long hours of clerical work but, whenever any precious free time became available, I made sure to spend it with friends, both naval and civilian, bathing and swimming off the superb beaches of Stanley Bay and Sidi Bishr, located to the east of the city.

The latter beach was the most frequented by us for, directly opposite it stood a very attractive private residence called 'La Verande'. This property belonged to a prominent Alexandria solicitor and my three close friends and myself had the good fortune to have become acquainted with Monsieur S, his charming wife and his two teenage daughters. Their home was always open to us and many were the joyful parties experienced there.

For us navy types, this was our first experience of a summer in the Middle East, where on most days the temperature hovered in the high eighties, with oppressive humidity. Yet despite this, a few diehards (including myself) would happily turn out for a few sets of tennis or for a cricket match. "Mad dogs and Englishmen go out in the midday sun!"

Unhappily, these diversions were occasionally interspersed with miserable bouts of sickness – usually an enervating intestinal complaint known as "Gippy Guts" – from which few of us remained unscathed. The only consolation with this illness was that, once afflicted a person's immune system seemed to resist repeat performances!

The beach at Sidi Bishr in the forties.

In late August I had the misfortune to land in hospital with a severe attack of *otitis media* – a most painful ear infection caused, according to our doctor, by excessive sea-bathing! It took four days of treatment, consisting mainly of boiling hot poultices being applied to both ears, until the build-up of infection burst. A most agonising procedure!

Before being discharged from hospital I was allowed four hours shore leave. This required the wearing of the very conspicuous regulation hospital patient's uniform, which consisted of an ill-fitting bright blue jacket and trousers, white shirt and a crimson tie. Kind friends insisted on taking me to tea and, despite my protestations, we finished up in the elegant Pastroudi's restaurant on Rue Fouad where, to my discomfort, I had to endure many compassionate glances from other guests who, obviously, believed me to be a battle casualty, back from the Western Desert front!

August 1941 – author (left) in hospital attire, being visited by a shipmate.

I recall that it was on the same day, after leaving this restaurant, that we encountered a most bizarre incident. We were making our way to the tram station when, suddenly, ahead of us appeared a large crowd of people, clustered outside a popular *patisserie* called Delices. This café was famous for its espresso coffee, accompanied by a mouth-watering choice of delicious meringues, mille-feuilles, chocolate éclairs, rum babas and other temptations, all laid out invitingly on large trays on the counters.

As we pushed our way through the crowd to see what was happening, we were confronted by the rear end of a horse, protruding through the hanging strands of coloured beads which covered the entrance. The remainder of the animal was inside and, as we craned our necks to get a better view of the interior, we were presented with an incredible sight.

The horse, surrounded by four hefty Australian soldiers, was happily munching away on all the cakes on the trays and, over by the cash-desk, another Aussie was calmly handing over wads of banknotes to the bewildered proprietor!

We then noticed, on the roadside, a *gharry* (horse-drawn taxi), minus the usual horse between the shafts. Speaking to one of the bystanders, we gathered that the Aussies (always sympathetic to things equestrian) had apparently been passengers in the *gharry* and had decided that the horse was ill-fed and, despite the protestations of the native driver, had abruptly stopped the vehicle, released the horse from its harness and led it into Delices for a feast of a lifetime! All being paid for with boodles of back-pay earned after weeks of active service in the front lines.

Ramleh Square, Alexandria in the 1940s.

This was one of the more harmless and amusing incidents that allied troops on leave would indulge in. More often, encounters of a more serious nature would erupt, usually between servicemen and civilians, and the ubiquitous military police patrols would speedily intervene to re-establish peace and good order. The local constabulary – the *'shawishes'* – always seemed to be quite content to stay clear of these fracas!

Back, once again, at the office, an interesting announcement appeared on the noticeboard. The Admiralty had introduced several new schemes for accelerated advancement for various rating categories. Leading Writers would now be permitted to sit the professional examination for Petty Officer after the completion of only six months in the lower grade.

In April, I had entered and passed the examination for Leading Writer. Now, here was a golden opportunity to further improve my financial status which, due to the increasing demands of my off-duty social activities, had resulted in the balance in my Post Office Savings Account teetering close to the zero mark.

So, exercising great resolve, I started to spend as much off-duty time as possible memorizing the myriads of forms promulgated by the Admiralty to deal with every possible naval contingency that could occur. Also, I managed to persuade two of my close colleagues to follow my example. This was a wily move, for it led to the three of us, together, holding sessions exchanging useful items of information rather than me, alone, attempting to study, whilst they would be suggesting more attractive pursuits! To assist in our endeavours, we were successful in borrowing a copy of the *Kings Regulations and Admiralty Instructions* – a hefty tome, irreverently referred to as 'The Bible' and a most essential *vade-mecum* for all matters naval.

As the year came to a close, some good news filtered through from the Western Desert. At last, after being besieged for almost twenty months, the port of Tobruk was relieved in early December. Almost simultaneously, however, came the bad news – this from the theatre of war in the Far East, where, off the east coast of Malaya, the RN battleships *Repulse* and *Prince of Wales* had both been sunk by Japanese aircraft operating from bases in Indo-China.

To add to the misery, we were shocked to learn that the Japanese, without any warning, had carried out a crippling attack on the United States Pacific Fleet at anchor in Pearl Harbor, sinking and damaging numerous vessels and causing almost four thousand casualties.

Needless to say, these items of news had a somewhat dampening effect on the Christmas festivities we had already begun to plan.

6.   Back to School

The year 1942 swept in, bringing with it the coldest weather experienced by the local populace in forty-odd years of recordkeeping. This tended to make life unpleasant as, both in our offices and in our lodgings, we had but meagre means of keeping warm, other than to don extra clothing and to pile on more blankets for sleeping. Outside pursuits were no longer so enticing, which, in a way, was a good thing, in that my two friends and myself – all aspiring Petty Officers – were more resigned to spending our off-duty time swotting hard for the forthcoming examination.

After two exasperating last-minute postponements, we were finally instructed to report to the Examining Officer at the naval base HMS *Nile* on January 30th.

After the exam, as we exchanged information as we returned to the B.A.O., we managed to convince each other that we had scraped through, but it was not until the end of February, when we were ushered into the presence of our Paymaster Captain, that we were finally notified of our successes.

That evening was given to celebrating and, a few days later, we were ordered to pack our belongings in readiness for a move into the senior ratings quarters, located in the Savoy Pension, a most imposing edifice close to the seafront and within close walking distance of the office.

The following Sunday we hastened to 'La Verande', where our ever-helpful Madame S busied herself sewing on our Petty Officer cap and sleeve badges and replacing our black buttons with the regulation 'gold' (actually gilt) buttons.

It was shortly after this promotion that the long-awaited 'flock' of W.R.N.S. ratings (Wrens) finally arrived, after a six-week voyage around the Cape from England. Most of these new arrivals were allocated for duties in the B.A.O. and I inherited six of them for the ledger section, of which I was now in charge. One or two of these newcomers were quite matronly, or so they seemed to me, a mere twenty-one year old! Once they had been instructed in the rudiments of their jobs, these women proved to be excellent and conscientious workers so that, very soon, those sections in the office where there was a backlog of work were brought up-to-date.

At around this time we were experiencing an increased frequency in air raid alerts, some of which were severe and long-lasting. Although Ras-el-Tin harbour was the main target, some bombs fell on the town, including one which landed quite close to our 'pension' and which did considerable damage to properties near the seafront.

Our Wrens took all this disturbance in their stride, most of them having had experience of enemy air-raids when they had been working in the naval bases of Chatham, Portsmouth, Devonport and others. However, what really upset them was their first taste of a *khamseen*, which occurred a few days after their arrival.

Khamseen is the Arabic word for 'fifty', and this is the approximate number of hot, sand-laden winds which blow in from the Sahara Desert in any one year. The more severe examples of this wind create a suffocating dirty blanket of air, which tends to hang over the city, blocking out the sun completely. It has often been referred to as "the ninth plague of Egypt." These windstorms usually sweep in without warning and, if one happens to be out of doors, the fine sand particles clog up eyes, nostrils and ears, whilst clothing assumes a dirty yellowish colour.

Early in April, having no longer any swotting to occupy my leisure hours, I decided to 'go back to school', especially as I now had some useful additional income at my disposal. On the outward voyage from England I had taken advantage of a series of classes, given as a preliminary introduction in the Arabic language by a fellow-passenger, a RAF officer who, prior to the war, had served in various Middle East postings. Now, after eighteen months in Egypt, I had to admit to myself that my knowledge of the language could only be described as rudimentary, so I decided to do something about it.

Making enquiries, I was pleased to discover that the world-famous Berlitz language school had a branch located in the city centre, not too distant from our 'pension'. On visiting the school I was informed that they had a course about to commence in Beginner's Arabic, which offered lessons twice weekly over period of two months.

The fee was reasonable and I decided to enrol, knowing that I was taking a gamble on whether I would still be stationed in Egypt for the foreseeable future. Also, I ignored the somewhat uncomplimentary remarks expressed by some of my fellow workers, who regarded me as being deranged for wanting to spend my free time in this manner.

The teacher for this course was an elderly Egyptian gentleman, well-educated and with a distinguished bearing. He spoke fluent French and also had a useful smattering of English. He presided over a mixed bag of twelve students, all male, representing various European nationalities but mostly French-speaking and, very soon, it became evident that his method of instruction was very thorough. Not only did he strive patiently to improve our vocabulary but also he went to great pains to ensure that we gained some knowledge of Muslim etiquette, which, we were to learn, involved most formal and elaborate politeness.

He explained that the open displays of gratitude and sympathy considered acceptable in European society were not expected when mingling with the residents of the countries of the Levant. For example, we learned that if, upon meeting an acquaintance, one enquired about the well-being of any of the women-folk of his household, this could be regarded as a grave discourtesy, being an intrusion into one's private affairs. Most definitely, "how are you, Bill, and how's the missus?" would be frowned upon!

Also, beware not to admire or compliment a friend's child on its good looks. This could land you in trouble if, for example, the said child later suffered a misfortune of some kind. Also, if visiting the home of one's acquaintance, refrain from openly admiring any of his possessions, as this could be interpreted as asking to be given them! If, whilst in that home, you were to be offered the customary 'demi-tasse' of syrupy Turkish coffee, the polite expression to use when taking a first sip would be *"daiman"* meaning 'always', the implication being "may you always be blessed with good things in your household." Beware, however, of saying this if, to your knowledge, there had been a recent death in the family!

If sitting in the company of others, our professor warned us, be careful not to allow the sole of your foot to face directly one or other of the persons present. Such a gesture was most definitely *'haram'* (not acceptable).

Gradually, as the weeks passed under the patient guidance of our long-suffering teacher, most of us made reasonable progress and I, personally, discovered that in my daily contacts with local shopkeepers and servants in our pension, I had ample opportunity to make practical use of my newly-acquired knowledge. Moreover, in the course of doing so, I encountered respect and helpfulness from most of the individuals with whom I had conversations, and, by hearing and imitating, I soon was able to communicate fairly intelligently on most simple everyday matters.

At the end of the course I purchased a text-book entitled *Colloquial Arabic* which had been strongly recommended by the professor, to enable me to continue with self-study.

There was no question in my mind that the cost of the course had been money well spent and, unbeknown to me at that time, it was to bring an unanticipated dividend within less than three years.

7. Un Coup de Foudre

It was shortly after I had become absorbed with my Arabic course that an event occurred that was to have an effect on my entire life.

It all started innocently enough one evening when, on arrival back at the pension, I was surprised to find a typewritten envelope marked 'Personal' addressed to me. It contained a neatly printed card from Paul R and it "requested the pleasure of my attendance" at a banquet and dance to be held at the Swiss Club at the end of April.

The following morning I telephoned Paul at his office, thanking him and confirming that I would very much like to attend but, knowing that for a soirée of this nature the guests would most likely be *en grande tenue,* I would have to come in uniform. Would that be acceptable? He promptly assured me that there was no need to worry on that score as it was almost certain that some of the other club members would also be inviting servicemen whom they had befriended.

So, the evening of April 25th (I well remember the date) found me sharing a table, laden with good fare, with Paul, his wife Lilli, and several members of his office staff, some of whom I had previously met. During the meal a four-piece orchestra provided pleasant background music. When the meal was over it was "all hands on deck" to assist in clearing the tables and chairs to make space for the dance-floor and when this was done, the band launched into the music for the first dance. It happened to be the Marie Elena waltz – I remember it well – and several couples immediately took to the floor.

I found myself standing alone, but it must have been less than two minutes before Paul appeared, quite suddenly, escorting a most attractive dark-haired young woman attired in a strikingly beautiful white ball-dress.

At first glance I could see, from her deportment, that she was of a good family – in fact she appeared to have a regal bearing but, even so, I was not expecting to hear Paul's opening remarks.

"Tom, I would very much like to introduce you to Princess Nahidé Kadjar," and, turning to the young beauty at his side, he explained, "Thomas Soars is a very good friend of mine from England. Before the war, he was an employee of the insurance company for which I am the representative here in Egypt."

I was completely taken aback, not knowing whether to bow respectfully or to shake hands but, fortunately, the Princess took the initiative by holding out a white-gloved hand for me to shake.

Then, boldly, I asked her, in French, as it was in this language that Paul had introduced her, if she would care to dance. Without any hesitation she acquiesced and, guiding her carefully by the arm, I led her out onto the dance floor.

As we merged into the swirl of dancing couples she enquired, in French, how long I had been in Egypt and during the course of the dance we exchanged the usual pleasantries. We chatted mostly in French but I also discovered that she had a fairly good knowledge of English which, she assured me, she was keen to improve.

During the course of that evening she took to the floor for almost every dance, again with myself, as well as with some of the young Swiss fellows present, with whom she appeared to be on friendly terms.

I also danced with some of the other ladies present and, towards the end of the evening, after one of these dances, I looked around for the princess but was unable to see her. Approaching my friend Paul, I enquired as to her whereabouts and he confirmed, to my chagrin, that she had just taken her leave, accompanied by a member of her family who had arrived to escort her home.

He noticed my disappointment.

"Don't worry," he said. "You'll probably have further opportunities to meet her."

"Tell me, Paul," I enquired. "Is she *really* a royal personage?"

"But of course," he replied. "A genuine Persian princess. Her father is a Prince of the old Kadjar ruling family of Persia. It so happens that her mother is a Swiss subject by birth and the family is highly regarded in our local community."

"I really enjoyed making her acquaintance, short as it was," I said. "But I doubt whether I'll ever have the pleasure of seeing her again."

"Oh, you never know…" replied Paul.

During the following days I had difficulty trying to keep this young lady out of my thoughts, and I had to keep reminding myself that the chances of renewing our brief acquaintance were extremely remote. Therefore, I was astounded when, three weeks later, I received a telephone call directly from her. She explained that she had been given my phone number by Paul and hoped that I did not object.

"On the contrary," I replied. "I'm delighted."

She explained that at the end of the month there was to be an open-air *soirée* at the Nouzha Gardens (a park on the outskirts of the city). It was being held on behalf of some charity.

"Would you like to come?" she enquired.

I agreed with alacrity!

Before the appointed evening arrived, I had an opportunity, during one of my regular visits to Paul's home, to learn more about the background of the Kadjar family. He informed me that Princess Nahidé was, in fact, the great grand-daughter of the dynamic Nasr-Ed-Din Shah, who had ruled Persia from 1848 until 1896 and had been the first Persian ruler ever to have visited England. This took place in the summer of 1873 when he and his large retinue were the guests of Queen Victoria at Buckingham Palace.

Princess Nahidé Sultan Kadjar, 1940.

The Kadjar dynasty had occupied the Persian throne from 1795 until 1925, when Ahmad Shah (Nahidé's cousin) had been deposed following a coup d'état engineered by Reza Khan, the Prime Minister at that time.

Ahmad's uncle, Prince Salar-ed-Dowleh (Nahidé's father), who was in Europe at the time of this usurpation, decided to return to his homeland in response to urgent appeals from pro-Kadjar elements. Crossing into western Persia from Iraq, he was successful in assembling a large force of several tribes loyal to his cause and advanced eastwards towards the capital, Tehran, defeating, en route, pro-Reza Khan's followers in several clashes.

Reza Khan appealed to the British Minister in Tehran for support and, as the government in London felt that British interests would be best served by assisting Reza, the order was given for R.A.F. planes to fly from bases in neighbouring Iraq. These planes scattered leaflets on the Prince's followers, urging them to disband or suffer the consequences of their villages being subjected to aerial bombardment. Reluctantly, to avoid bloodshed and suffering for his adherents, the Prince abandoned his eastward advance. Later, he was trapped by a British patrol as he crossed the frontier back into Iraq and, solely to placate the usurper to the Persian throne, he was taken to Baghdad and placed under house arrest.

After several months of detention, without legal warrant, the British High Commissioner for Iraq, embarrassed by enquiries made by high-ranking friends of the Prince, arranged for him to be transported to British-occupied Palestine, where he was joined by his family. There they lived in a villa at Bath Gelim, on the outskirts of Haifa. This villa was adjacent to a British Military camp, where a close watch could be maintained on the family's comings and goings.

It was not until 1934 that the Prince was finally freed from this exile – and then only on condition that he would not attempt to re-enter his homeland. Instead, he and his family were allowed to move to Alexandria, after permission to reside there had been given by Egypt's King Fouad.

After listening to Paul's lengthy account concerning Nahidé's family's odyssey I was left feeling somewhat embarrassed, but at the same time sceptical, regarding the role of my own government in this affair. Many years later I would have the opportunity to delve into this history, when I spent almost two weeks visiting daily the Public Records Office at Kew, near London. There, poring over original documents taken from the archives of the British Legation in Tehran, I was able to confirm the accuracy of the events carefully outlined to me by my Swiss friend.

Before taking my leave that evening, I mentioned to Paul that I had received a telephone call from the Princess, inviting me to the Nouzha Gardens event, but he did not appear unduly surprised at this news. This convinced me that he had undoubtedly been cross-examined by the family as to my credentials and back-ground and, evidently, had been successful in setting their minds at rest on both counts!

Counting the days, I eagerly looked forward to a second meeting with the charming young lady with whom I had been so impressed during our all-too-brief encounter at the Swiss club.

At last, around the middle of June, we met again. This time she was looking more beautiful than ever and was accompanied by one of her sisters. Also present that evening were some of the Swiss people with whom I was already acquainted.

The soirée was a tremendous success and, despite quite intense competition, I managed to partner Nahidé for several dances. It was during one of these that she had insisted on my addressing her by her christian name, and she, in turn, called me Thomas.

The evening passed all too quickly and eventually, it came time for the two Princesses to depart – they were to be driven home by a Swiss family with whom, I gathered, they had a long-standing close relationship. Before leaving, Nahidé thanked me for a delightful evening and murmured, "I do hope that we will be able to meet again soon. I have your phone number and will contact you before the end of the month."

With that, she joined her sister in the back seat of the car.

As I watched it drive off and disappear into the night I had no way of knowing that a disastrous turn of events on the war front during the next two weeks would render it highly unlikely that we would ever meet again.

8. Evacuation

By the time I had completed my Arabic course in early June the war situation had so deteriorated that it seemed to me quite possible that to be able to make use of the language in Egypt was becoming rather a dim prospect.

The news from the front line was extremely disconcerting. Rommel's forces had succeeded in getting strong reinforcements through from bases in southern Sicily and, by the end of May, had resumed the offensive, recapturing Tobruk three weeks later. Then, despite stubborn resistance by the Allied troops, the enemy had managed to advance eastwards, penetrating into Egyptian territory as far as the small village of El Alamein, only sixty miles from Alexandria's western city limits. En route, Rommel had captured an enormous amount of Allied material – in fact it was estimated that by the time he had reached El Alamein, over 75% of his transport vehicles were spoils of war.

Learning of the proximity of the enemy, unrest broke out in the city and we learned that some of the more shrewd members of the population were busy making preparations to welcome the 'victorious' German and Italian forces when they reached the outskirts.

Rommel, himself, broadcast an announcement that he was "pursuing the conquered British forces all the way back to the Nile". Jumping on the bandwagon, Hitler's junior partner, the Italian dictator, Mussolini, had himself flown to the port of Derna (well away from the front line), where he spent several days planning theatrical preparations for his triumphal entry into Cairo and, it was rumoured, had left instructions back in Rome for special medals to be minted to commemorate 'The Italian Occupation of Egypt'!

While mobs were openly cheering for Rommel in the streets of Cairo, we heard that the staff at the British Embassy were engaged in burning official documents and planning evacuation procedures.

In Alexandria all shore establishments were put on alert. This included the B.A.O., where it became "all hands on deck" to pack up all the office equipment and records and to be ready, at short notice, for a speedy withdrawal.

By the late afternoon of June 30th the entire male staff was en route to the dockyard, there to be embarked on a freighter, the S.S. *Antwerp*, along with the personnel from several other shore establishments. Our Wrens were not with us. We were informed that "for safety reasons" they were being evacuated by road. This sounded rather ominous.

That evening we sailed out of the harbour in a convoy and proceeded in an easterly direction to an undisclosed destination. During the night we came under U-Boat attack and, as we listened to the distant explosions of depth-charges, we appreciated why the authorities had decided to send the Wrens by road.

We spent a sleepless night standing around below deck, wearing lifejackets, and it was a relief when, in the early morning light, we were all allowed on deck, there to see the familiar lighthouse, with the De Lesseps statue standing beyond, guarding the entrance to the Suez Canal.

We had arrived in Port Said, but was this our destination or merely a port of call?

It was made clear, when a pinnace came out from Navy House, that we were to disembark here and, some time later, the ship was ordered to a jetty where we laboured to unload all our personal baggage and the office files and equipment. After this strenuous effort we were taken to the naval barracks, there to enjoy a much appreciated breakfast, following which we again boarded the lorries to be transported to our new place of employment. This turned out to be a theatre which had been requisitioned by the Admiralty to be used as both the office and our living quarters. Our Wrens, we were sad to learn, were to be accommodated elsewhere!

Port Said, entrance to the Suez Canal.

I was fortunate enough to be able to move my belongings into one of several small dressing-rooms located behind the stage. These were devoid of furniture but were relatively clean and, surprisingly, equipped with a wash-basin with a mirror over it and running water.

The rest of that day was fully occupied with the unloading and setting up of all our office gear and, that evening, exhausted after the previous sleepless night, everyone was pleased to turn in early.

Having nowhere to hang my hammock, I spread it out on the floor of my room and stripped to my shorts and singlet. I did not bother with any covering as it was very warm. In no time I fell into a deep sleep.

I awakened with the early morning light filtering through the tiny window and, as I gradually regained consciousness, I became aware of a vague movement across my midriff. Looking down, I was spellbound to see a large army of black ants marching in close formation from under the door, crossing over the "mountain" – which happened to be me – and continuing in their relentless progression across the floor to disappear through a hole in the skirting-board on the opposite wall!

Author with Sudanese caretaker of the theatre where we were billeted.

Fortunately, I had the presence of mind to remain motionless until, finally, the rearguard of the contingent disappeared down the hole. Had I acted otherwise there would have been masses of disoriented ants everywhere and, for all I knew, they could have been of the biting variety! Later, I told the Sudanese caretaker who, it appeared, had been acquired with the theatre, to do "something about it." I never found out exactly what action he had taken but, after that episode, I had no more trouble from marching ants!

A day or two later our Wrens arrived, in a sorry state, their normally trim white uniforms dirty and dishevelled after long weary hours of travel in the backs of none-too-clean lorries. They were all very upset with the 'powers that be' for not being allowed to travel with us by sea. However, they very soon forgot about this miserable experience after a few days in Port Said, enjoying its many off-duty diversions – dances at the Casino Palace Hotel, teas at Simon Artz, movies at the Empire and, last but not least, Gianola's popular ice-cream bar.

These halcyon days were destined to be of short duration, however, for towards the end of July we received news of a deteriorating situation in the Western Desert and this, coupled with an increasing number of enemy air-raids on the harbour and dockyard areas, prompted the C-in-C to order the B.A.O. to prepare for yet another move, this time further south, away from the Med altogether.

We were all beginning to wonder just *how* far south!

On the first day of August, still unaware of our ultimate destination, we once again went through our packing procedure. Early the following morning naval transport took us to the railway station, where we boarded a train bound for Port Tewfik, at the southern end of the Suez Canal, about ninety miles distant. This was where I had landed, almost two years ago, after the long sea journey around the Cape from England. During the train trip rumours were rife that perhaps we were going as far south as Cape Town, or maybe Mombasa in Kenya?

That evening the conjectures of the optimists were rudely dashed, for on arrival in the evening we were not transported to a ship in the harbour but to a school – empty for the summer recess – on the outskirts of the town. There, toiling in oppressive heat, we went through the now familiar procedure of 'setting up shop'.

Scrounging around, we managed to find camp-beds and some mattresses, which the male staff set up next to our work stations, while the Wrens were able to use a dormitory in the annexe.

The first nights were uncomfortable for those using the mattresses, which they found they were sharing with colonies of bed-bugs. Also, we had to become accustomed to sleeping under mosquito-nets, which were essential this far south.

There was one consolation. In the school grounds we found a rather dilapidated tennis court, enabling the more energetic souls amongst us to play a few sets in the cool of the evenings.

Several members of the staff became sick, mostly with the accursed *Gippy Tummy*, and some of the more serious cases finished up in the naval hospital in Port Suez, where – we were saddened to learn later – one of our Wrens died from typhoid fever and two others with serious illnesses were invalided back home to the UK.

When visiting Suez we were cheered to see the tremendous build-up of tanks and other war material being unloaded from freighters, which had been arriving frequently after sailing in convoy the twelve-thousand-mile long supply route from English ports. At any one time we could count as many as a hundred vessels, either at anchor or alongside the jetties. To protect against air attacks, this armada was under a vast panoply of barrage balloons.

News of this colossal build-up of both men and material had, no doubt, reached an anxious Rommel, through secret agents. He was still bogged down at El Alamein, waiting for Hitler to send him the promised reinforcements to enable him to push through to the Canal. However, an incredible thing happened, there was a change of plan by German High Command and these reinforcements were diverted to the Russian front.

Nevertheless, at the end of August, Rommel decided on a desperate gamble and launched a full-scale attack, hoping to out-flank the allied defensive positions, but General Montgomery's Eighth Army stubbornly stood its ground and eventually forced the enemy to withdraw, with heavy losses. Montgomery, wisely, did not counter-attack. He knew that he had time on his side.

A few days later, orders came through from Alexandria for the B.A.O. to return there. Once again we packed all our gear onto lorries and travelled with it to the railway station, there to board an early morning train to Cairo. Most of us took advantage of a three hour stop-over there to look around the city in the vicinity of the station, and managed to make a quick visit to the famous Groppis restaurant for coffee and cakes.

That evening we were glad to arrive back in our old quarters in Alexandria, where we were greeted as returning heroes by our civilian friends, who went out of their way to arrange joyful reunion parties in the following days. We could well understand their relief at seeing us again; since the end of June they had faced the unpleasant possibility of the city falling to the enemy forces.

To further enhance the new mood of confidence, a visiting ENSA troupe, which included Harry Tate, Alice Delysia, Carl Carlyle and others, put on a splendid variety show for our benefit.

It was good to be back home!

9. An Unexpected Escapade

On the morning of October 23rd 1942 Alexandrians awakened to the sound of distant rumbling of heavy artillery fire punctuated by the noise of exploding bombs. This continued uninterrupted throughout the day and then into the night when intermittent flashes on the western horizon became clearly visible.

Although we did not realize it at that time, what had just commenced was to become renowned in military history as the Battle of El Alamein.

Later, we learned that the allied attack on a four-mile front had been closely coordinated with both air and naval support pounding the enemy's lengthy supply line, stretching westwards along the entire coastal highway. Simultaneously, enemy convoys carrying much-needed oil, ammunition and reinforcements from Italian and Sicilian ports had been destroyed by allied naval and air attacks before they could reach safe harbour in Tripoli – the one-time pride of Mussolini's Colonial Empire.

Despite stubborn resistance, the Afrika Korps and its Italian allies were being routed with heavy losses and, by mid-November, had been swept completely out of Egyptian territory. Prisoners had been rounded up in their thousands and sent, under armed guard, on the long eastward journey to the outskirts of Alexandria, there to be incarcerated in several hastily-prepared compounds.

En route they had to pass through a veritable graveyard of wrecked tanks, guns and transports, interspersed with hastily-dug last resting-places for some of the many fallen.

At about this time another memorable event, one of a much more personal nature, also occurred. I was surprised to receive a telephone call from Nahidé Kadjar, whom I last had the pleasure of seeing at the Nouzha Gardens dance, just a short while before I had become part of the Navy's full-scale exodus from Alexandria.

She said that she had been advised by our mutual friend, Paul R that I had returned to Alexandria. We had quite a lengthy conversation, at the end of which I ventured to ask if I could have her telephone number but, politely, she declined to give me this but promised that she would get into touch with me again as soon as she could find 'a suitable opportunity'. I surmised that the term 'suitable opportunity' implied an occasion when she could arrange to call me without her parents' knowledge!

True to her word, ten days later she phoned again and I had the temerity to invite her and her sister out to tea. She accepted my invitation and suggested we meet at a small, discreet restaurant called *Au Petit Sevigne*, located in the down-town area.

This was to become the first of a regular routine of clandestine trysts using this particular rendezvous. Our friendship continued to blossom with each meeting and, in spite of our completely different backgrounds, we gradually discovered that we had many interests in common.

Nahidé was fond of animals, especially dogs. So was I. She liked the outdoors, especially to be near the sea. So did I. She preferred alfresco picnics on the beach to restaurant meals. So did I. She was keen to improve her English – and I my French. So we had fun helping each other linguistically.

The time spent in her company became very precious to me. So much so that when, at the end of November, our Paymaster-Lieutenant advised me that, as I had now been on foreign service for more than two years, I was eligible to apply for home leave, I decided against making such application, much to that officer's surprise.

In lieu of home leave I was entitled to take time off locally, so I decided to spend a few days on a sight-seeing visit to Cairo and, at the same time, to keep a long-standing promise to visit Eddie S who was Paul's manager of the company there. I had been introduced to him and his delightful wife and baby daughter when, the previous year they had vacationed in Alexandria.

When I mentioned my intentions to Nahidé, she had a brainwave.

"I have some close friends living in Heliopolis, a Cairo suburb, and for some time they have been pressing me to pay them a visit. If my parents agree to my going there for a few days then I will see if I can arrange it so that I'll be there at the same time as you. That is, of course, if you would like that," she added.

"Like it?" I replied. "It sounds like a splendid idea! But are you quite certain that you'll be able to get your family's consent to go alone?"

"Now that I'm almost twenty-one – I will be in less than two months – I feel sure that I'll get them to agree." She looked so determined as she said this that I was confident she could overcome any objections!

Two or three days after this conversation, she phoned to confirm that all was arranged and that she had spoken to her Cairo friends, who had gladly invited her to stay with them whenever she decided to visit. Immediately upon receiving this news, I submitted my request for seven days leave, commencing on the 22nd December. It was approved and then, after conferring with Nahidé and making arrangements with my friends in Cairo, I made the necessary reservations for Pullman accommodation on the train.

I spent the days leading up to our departure working like a Trojan on my office section, making certain that everything would be 'ship-shape' by the time I left. I also arranged for a fellow Petty Officer to keep a watchful eye on my section during my absence, as there was always the possibility that one or other of the destroyers, for whose pay accounts I was responsible, would put into port without prior warning.

Usually such arrivals involved a visit to the ship in order to deal with various kinds of pay queries by crew members. Sometimes, these visits could be rather onerous in that, after all the paperwork was dealt with, there followed the habitual socializing – a drink or two in the wardroom or the senior ratings' mess – often in both!

I can recollect such encounters in the past where, on leaving a ship, I had experienced a certain difficulty in navigating the gang-plank down to the jetty whilst carrying a large bundle of ledgers under one arm!

On the morning of the twenty-second, Nahidé and I made our separate ways to Alexandria Station and met under the clock, as pre-arranged. We spent most of the 130-mile journey enjoying an extended lunch in the Pullman car, whilst taking in the fascinating lush scenery of the Nile delta region. The time passed quickly and, at around four in the afternoon, the train slowed as we approached a large sign marked *El Qahira*. We had reached Cairo.

Nahidé's friends were waiting to greet her and, after being introduced, we made arrangements to meet later in the evening at the National Hotel. We then went our separate ways – I taking a taxi for the short trip to the Garden City suburb of Bab-el-Luq where my friends lived in an attractive apartment building overlooking the Nile.

The ensuing six days were filled to the full as we made a point of visiting everything of interest. There was so much to be seen in this teeming city, which boasted the largest population in Africa.

We spent almost an entire day wandering around the Museum of Egyptian Antiquities, where we were enthralled by the priceless collections of artefacts, representing a cultured and prosperous civilization which existed thousands of years before Christ was born; at a time when, in my own part of the world, my ancestors were, most probably, eking out a precarious life as cave dwellers.

Nahidé, outside a hotel in Cairo.

Another day, my Swiss friends, to whom I had introduced Nahidé, drove us out to view the world-famous pyramids at Ghizeh, south-west of the city. I marvelled at these colossal man-made constructions of the ancient world. The largest one, the tomb of the Pharaoh named Cheops, had a base covering an area of over twelve acres and was built using limestone blocks, each block, according to our guide, weighing in excess of two tons. Adjacent to these monuments was the world-renowned Sphinx, which depicts the head of the Pharaoh surmounted on the reclining body of a lion.

After lunch at the nearby Mena House Hotel we drove south along a desert highway for about fifteen miles until we arrived at the much older, but not so impressive, pyramids of Saquara, located close to the ruins of Memphis, the ancient capital city of Egypt. Returning to Cairo, we took the picturesque riverside road that runs along the west bank of the Nile.

Another memorable day saw us boarding an early morning train that took us to The Barrage, the dam which straddles the river about thirteen miles north of the city. We took a picnic lunch with us and ate this in green parkland, reminiscent of England.

Later, for only a few piastres, we were able to hire a rowboat in which we ventured out on the river, taking care to stay clear of the numerous busy *dhows*, plying their cargoes up and down this historic waterway.

Despite these energetic daytime excursions, we both found that we still possessed sufficient vigour for evening sorties. We danced at the National Hotel, went to one or other of the several open-air cinemas, most of which were showing the latest Hollywood movies, and enjoyed quiet dinners at Groppis, where, less than four months previously, I had snatched a quick coffee and cakes during my stop-over between trains on BAO's return journey to Alexandria after our enforced 'exile' in Tewfik.

Fortunately, at that time of the year Cairo's climate was relatively cool and dry. At any other time we would have found it physically impossible to have packed in such a busy schedule in so short a period.

Nahidé rowing on the Nile.

All too soon, our brief escapade came to an end and we were back on the train, bound for Alexandria. After a light lunch, Nahidé nodded off, but I remained awake, my mind recalling details of the happy hours we had shared during the last few days. Studying the reposed, sleeping face opposite to me, I asked myself if I was really doing the right thing in becoming so involved with this delightful person. Deep inside of me I had this feeling that I was falling in love but, I asked myself, was this all merely a pipe-dream? Was I being irrational to ever imagine – considering the huge gulf of family, culture and nationality between us – that a permanent relationship could ever be possible?

I was still pondering this dilemma when I felt the train's motion gradually slowing for its final approach to our destination. Nahidé awakened and, seeing the outskirts of the city, realized that our venture was nearing its end.

She must have read my thoughts, for she said, "It's been a wonderful holiday and I'm sure that we'll find a way to do it again."

As previously arranged, we said our farewells before the train pulled into its platform so that, on arrival, we could once again go our separate ways. I assisted her with her suitcase to a waiting taxi, then boarded the next car in line.

Thus our first vacation together came to an end.

10. Affianced ~ and Godparents!

The year 1943 started off, so far as the war was concerned, not with a bang but with a definite promise of a bang when, in January, the allied heads of state, with their military advisers, all met in Casablanca, Morocco. At that memorable meeting the Allies agreed to commence the joint planning necessary for the next phase of the campaign – the invasion of Sicily and the Italian mainland. This was to be a lengthy procedure and did not actually take place until the beginning of July.

Meanwhile, in Alexandria, other memorable happenings of a more personal nature were occurring. On the twenty-first of February Nahidé and I decided, after much deliberation, to become engaged. Only a few very close friends were made aware of this decision.

In that same month, Nahidé was approached by one of her family's Swiss friends to see if she would be interested in taking on a job. The position available was that of Directrice of a home which provided counselling and shelter for a limited number of young, backward, forward or wayward girls. The Swiss community was very active in promoting various *oeuvres de bienfaisance*, one of which was this 'Bureau de Protection des Enfants'.

Nahidé, being keen on social service work, was eager to take the appointment, but was rather doubtful as to whether her parents would readily give their approval. Fortunately, the very forceful matron, Mme B, who headed the committee responsible for this charitable venture, was held in high regard by Nahidé's family who, after being given full details of the duties involved, overcame their initial reluctance and gave their permission for their daughter to assume this responsibility.

Nahidé tackled the post with energy and enthusiasm. Within a relatively short time she made several improvements regarding the manner in which the home was administered and, more importantly, she was able to gain respect and support from both the small domestic staff and the residents. Her involvement became very apparent to me when, after regaling me with a sumptuous lunch, which she had prepared herself, she suddenly announced, "How would you like to become a godfather?"

Never before having been requested to consider such a liability, I decided to navigate with caution and, before committing myself, asked for further details.

Apparently, one of the young inmates had quite recently given birth to a daughter, the father being a British serviceman who had belatedly married the girl but had then been transferred with his unit to Syria, from where he had been unable to obtain compassionate leave to be present at the child's christening. Nahidé had already made up her mind to step in as the god-mother but nobody was available to fulfil the male role. Hence the question!

I was not all that enthusiastic about the idea but, not wishing to disappoint my fiancée, I agreed to assume the task. I had little conception of what was in store for me!

When the appointed day arrived for the ceremony, I sallied forth clad in my 'tiddly' (best) suit and, carrying a large bunch of flowers which Nahidé had asked me to bring, I arrived at the Greek Orthodox Church which had been chosen for the occasion.

I recollected that, one or two years before the war, I had been invited to attend a christening in my home town in England and this, I was about to find out, was a staid affair compared to the elaborate ritual now awaiting me!

Presided over by a richly-robed cleric of austere bearing, the small assembly, consisting of staff and inmates of the home, were requested to join in prolonged praying and singing prior to the actual baptism.

I was totally unprepared for what happened next. The unsuspecting infant, who had been blissfully asleep, was rudely awakened, stripped of its clothing and then, instead of the traditional gentle sprinkling, was subjected to a sustained ducking in the font. Finally, the long-suffering youngster was rescued by its mother and, without any artificial respiration, was dabbed dry with a towel before being dressed in its best clothes.

"Well I'm glad *that's* over," I murmured to myself, with considerable relief, but this turned out to be premature thinking!

All the persons present were handed large, yellow, lighted candles by the priest's assistant and lined up in single file. In readiness, I was informed, for the customary procession around the interior of the church. Before the 'quick march' command was given, I, being the godfather, was singled out to carry the infant – in addition to my lighted candle – and placed at the head of the procession, beside the priest. To complicate matters, the child, still fretting from its recent immersion, decided to take an immediate dislike to me and raised hell during the ensuing perambulation.

I have always prided myself that I managed to survive this unanticipated ordeal without dropping a single blob of candle-wax – either on my recently-acquired godchild or my best suit!

After it was all over, I received congratulations from those present but later, in a quiet aside to Nahidé, I complained that I had been quiet unprepared for such an arduous undertaking.

"You shouldn't grumble," she replied. "It could have been worse."

"How?" I asked.

With a mischievous grin, she retorted, "The baby could have peed on you!"

11. Back to Blighty

Now that the threat of enemy occupation had been decisively eradicated, the day-to-day life of Alexandria resumed a more relaxed tempo. Air-raids had become just an ugly memory and, by the middle of the year, allied convoys were able to sail, unmolested, from the Eastern Mediterranean right through to Gibraltar.

The harbour, by this time, was virtually congested with ships of all classes, laden with invasion material, waiting for the signal to commence the east-bound voyage to join in the three-pronged invasion of the island of Sicily. The other two armadas were to sail from various Algerian ports and also from the United Kingdom. D-day for the invasion was set for July 10th, and more than fifteen hundred ships and landing craft were being assembled in these ports in preparation for the initial landings.

Despite gale force winds and heavy seas, rendering landing conditions in some areas extremely hazardous, the Allies were successful in overcoming fierce enemy resistance and, by the middle of August, had driven the Germans and their reluctant allies out of Sicily completely. This defeat, and the knowledge that the Allies were now poised to invade the Italian mainland, caused serious unrest in Rome and the resignation of dictator Mussolini.

On September 9th the front pages of all the morning editions of Egyptian daily newspapers carried electrifying headlines, which announced that the Italian government had surrendered unconditionally and that all units of their fleet had been given orders to proceed immediately to British-held ports for internment.

Arriving at the office that morning, I found the entire staff all agog, discussing details of this astounding news and it was only with great difficulty that, eventually, everyone got down to their mundane daily tasks.

Later, that same morning, I was to be given some more exciting news. I was summoned to the office of the Paymaster Captain, there to be informed that, in view of my excellent record and rapid advancement through the ranks to Petty Officer, I was being recommended as a suitable C.W. candidate, for possible promotion to commissioned officer. The interview was of short duration but, as I was returning to my section, I was able to have a word with Chief Writer J.D., who was responsible for much of the paperwork in the Captain's office. He was aware of the reason why I had been seeing the Captain and congratulated me. Also, at my request, he 'filled me in' with more details and explained also that it was now simply a matter of waiting (and it could take some time) for a signal to arrive from the Admiralty confirming when I should be discharged to a Home Port prior to appearing before an Admiralty Selection Board.

"After that," he added, "provided you are able to convince the Board that you are, indeed 'officer material', you'll be packed off to HMS *King Alfred* to undergo a three-month training course, which, I've been told, is quite a strenuous undertaking."

I spent the remainder of that day agonising in my mind about this unexpected turn of events. On the one hand there was a feeling of immense satisfaction to have been offered this opportunity for promotion, but at the same time there was the realization that this would mean parting company with Nahidé – and for how long a period?

That evening, when I informed her of this development, she received the news with surprising stoicism. Instead of expressing dismay, as I had anticipated, she was delighted to learn that I had been given this chance for advancement. Nevertheless, I could see that she was putting on a brave face, so, in an attempt to soften the blow, I said, "I've been told that it could take a considerable time before I actually receive orders to leave and, who knows, the way the war is progressing, hostilities could be over by the end of the year."

She brightened up at this prospect, but I knew that I was being overoptimistic and unfair to build up false hopes, so I added, "You know, I don't have to go through with it. I can quite easily arrange to have my name withdrawn and to remain at the B.A.O. in my present job as long as possible."

After a moment's silence she replied, "No, you must not miss this opportunity. I'm sure you will be successful and, once you become an officer you'll have to return to Egypt."

She possessed far more optimism than I did. First of all, I was well aware that I could flunk the A.S.B. or fail to pass the subsequent training course. On the other hand, if I happened to make the grade, the odds were definitely against my returning to the Eastern Mediterranean. It was far more likely that I would be posted to a different theatre of war, quite possibly the Far East.

Also, on reflection, I had to admit to myself that, even if I were to elect to remain in my present duties, there was, of course, no guarantee that, sooner or later, I would not be transferred elsewhere.

The other possible solution, which we had considered when the signal first arrived, was for me to apply to get married, but from enquiries made, such an application would have taken some time for approval and, furthermore, Nahidé decided that her parents, at that stage, would not be in favour of our union.

So we simply decided to make the most of our remaining time together and were fortunate in that this turned out to be almost three months. It was not until the last week in

November when, at the office one morning, I was handed the B.A.O.'s copy of a signal addressed from the Admiralty to the C-in-C Levant, confirming that "Petty Officer T.H. Soars be discharged at the earliest opportunity to Royal Naval Barracks, Portsmouth for interview by the Admiralty Selection Board."

Following receipt of this message I was instructed to make myself ready to depart at short notice – which implied possibly just hours. Mindful of the memorable words of Cecil Rhodes – "So much to do and so little time to do it in" – I set about making my preparations for a rapid departure.

At the office, I had to instruct a colleague into the intricacies of my particular pay section whilst my free time became a frenzied round of farewell parties arranged by our mutual friends once they became aware of my impending departure.

As it happened, I was spared some respite in that it took longer than expected before, on December 13th, I received instructions to repair on board a destroyer, which was due to leave that same day for its home port, Portsmouth.

After a last telephone conversation with Nahidé I was taken in a naval transport, together with my kitbag, hammock and suitcase) down to the dockyard where, after a brief search, I located my ship, which was already preparing to get under way. I reported to the Officer of the Watch, who was not at all pleased to receive a last minute passenger.

I was not to be a passenger for long, however. No sooner had the shoreline receded into the distance than I was rounded up for duties in the ship's office where, throughout the voyage home, I was kept busy, using an ancient typewriter, producing all types of ship's forms and returns, most of which were long overdue.

However, this chore had two compensations. Firstly, I was able to sling my hammock in the privacy of the small office instead of in the crowded mess and, secondly, being kept so occupied, I had less time to dwell on the task which lay ahead of me. Also, I had the use of the typewriter, plus plenty of paper, to write a daily note to Nahidé – these accumulated notes to be mailed as soon as we reached our destination.

Before leaving we had promised to write to each other as often as possible and I had given her my sister's address, not being sure of where I would be located once I was back in England.

It was rumoured on board that if all went well we could arrive in Blighty by Christmas Day, but this was not to be. After several days of uneventful sailing, instead of calling in at Malta, as had been anticipated, we suddenly changed course to a north-westerly direction, leaving the crew speculating that our orders may have been changed and, instead of going home, we had been redirected to assist in the Allied landings on the Italian mainland.

This, so far as I was concerned, could be a worrying setback, as it would mean a delay in presenting myself before the Admiralty Selection Board.

Our destination was finally revealed when I was awakened one morning by the noisy clattering of anchor cables and, rushing up on deck, I discovered that we were in a harbour facing a large port. Looming in the background was an impressive, conical-shaped, mountain, from the summit of which, lazy wisps of black smoke were silhouetted against a blue sky. We had arrived in Catania and I was gazing at the famous Mount Etna.

Two days were spent in the harbour whilst some supplies were unloaded and taken to the naval base. It was here, less than five months ago, that elite units of the enemy had put up a stubborn resistance, impeding the advance of General Montgomery's troops up the Sicilian east coastal road. The navy had been called upon to assist and a battleship, escorted by cruisers and destroyers, had carried out a prolonged and punishing bombardment, which had devastated all the German military installations concentrated in this key town. This enabled the Eighth Army to continue its progress and link up a few days later with the American troops (which had advanced simultaneously along the north coast) at Messina, there to prepare for the crossing of the straits to the mainland of Italy. This completed the first stage in the liberation of the European continent.

After leaving Catania, we sailed directly through to the Atlantic and, on 5th January 1944, under an overcast sky and a heavy drizzle, our journey came to an end in Portsmouth harbour.

Several lorries were waiting to take the crew and their gear to the nearby barracks. On the way, I was to discover that it was a much-battered city compared to the Portsmouth to which I had travelled, almost four years previously, in order to volunteer to join the Navy.

12. Prelude to *King Alfred*

Thankfully, I only had to spend one uncomfortable night in the Petty Officers' mess in the naval barracks. The following morning, when I reported to the Drafting Office, I was presented with a rail travel voucher and informed that, having been on foreign service for three years, I was entitled to three weeks home leave. Whilst the prospect of leave was definitely appealing, I was anxious to appear before the Admiralty Selection Board with as little delay as possible but, upon further enquiry, I discovered that the next Board interviews were scheduled for the end of March. At the same time I was advised that these Boards were not held in Portsmouth, as I had assumed, but in Hove, Sussex.

So, after placing my heavy baggage in storage, I managed to get a lift to the station and was soon aboard a packed train, bound for Waterloo. The previous evening I had telephoned my sister who, since I had last seen her in October 1940, had married and was living in Gillingham, Kent. She had been expecting to hear from me, for in my last letter to her before leaving Egypt, I had made vague references that I could be soon arriving on her doorstep. She was delighted to hear my voice and welcomed me to stay at her home as long as I needed.

Gazing through the train window, I found it invigorating to see the familiar English countryside once again and, after leaving behind the city suburbs, there appeared to be surprisingly little evidence of the results of enemy bombing until we approached Clapham Junction. There we slackened speed and, until our arrival at Waterloo, the devastation on both sides of the railway track was very evident.

I descended to the Underground for the short trip to London Bridge Station where, finding that I had a wait of about forty minutes for the next Gillingham train, I decided to go for a stroll around the immediate precincts of the station. There were signs of extensive bomb damage everywhere I looked, except that, across the river, I was thrilled to see that the central dome of St Paul's Cathedral was standing unscathed, like a defiant national symbol amongst the ruins of so many of the surrounding buildings.

Arriving in Gillingham, I was fortunate enough to find one of the rare taxis and, within a few minutes, I was enjoying a happy reunion with my sister and her husband. Although I had managed to keep up correspondence with my sister during my absence, we found that there was still a lot of news to be exchanged and much midnight oil was burned in the process! Later during my leave, I spent some time travelling around Kent and Sussex, calling to see pre-war acquaintances. Sadly, in some cases I was only able to see grieving parents whose sons had become casualties in various theatres of war since I had last enjoyed their company.

I also paid a visit to the Brighton office of the insurance company where I had laboured before 1940 and the management and staff gave me quite a hero's welcome!

The time passed all too rapidly and, by the end of January, I returned to the barracks. Being a supernumerary, awaiting to be called before the Selection Board, I had no fixed duties and was allowed to live 'ashore' on condition that I checked into the barracks by 0800 hours each day, to see if there were any jobs of a temporary nature in which I could be of assistance. I soon found a comfortable room at the local Toc H with breakfast and an evening meal provided.

It was not until the third week in March that I joined up with a group of other C.W. candidates when, complete with kitbags and hammocks, we were taken to Portsmouth Harbour Station for the trip to Hove where, we assumed, we would report to H.M.S. *King Alfred*. Instead, we found two naval lorries awaiting us at Hove Station and we were taken on a tour through the residential district, until we pulled up before a red brick school building on Dyke Road. This school had been taken over by the Admiralty as an adjunct to *King Alfred*, to be used for various administrative purposes, including the A.S.B. sittings, and was located about two miles inland from "K.A." which was on the seafront at the west end of Hove.

No accommodation was available at the school, instead it was arranged for the candidates to be billeted in nearby private homes.

We were called upon in batches over the next few days, to appear before the A.S.B. When my turn came I was directed to a room with a group of other hopefuls, where an efficient Wren clerk explained to us that when we heard our names called from an adjoining room we were to enter by a door which she indicated.

There was a distinct air of nervousness as, one by one, my fellow candidates' names were called and they disappeared into the interview room, never to reappear, thus preventing any possibility for those waiting to question them on how the interviews were being conducted. After what seemed like ages, my name was called and I entered the room, where I found myself confronted by a most intimidating array of gold braid and decorations!

Seated at a long table covered with a green baize cloth were four very senior officers who, judging from my estimate of their ages, had probably been cajoled out of retirement to officiate on these boards. I was invited to sit in the lonely chair facing these awe-inspiring gentlemen and, immediately, the officer on the extreme left of the group launched into a series of questions, most of which were of a general nature pertaining to my schooling and pre-war activities, particularly sports, and my experience to date since joining the service. Judging from his facial expression, I got the distinct impression that he was not all that impressed.

He finished his interrogation and passed me to the officer next to him. This gentleman's questioning was of a more combative nature.

"Why is it," he enquired, "that you ask to be considered for an Executive Special Branch commission, when you have spent over three years in the Writer Branch?"

I explained that in 1940, when I had volunteered for naval service, I was only able to get accepted in that category but now that I was presented with an opportunity to change my occupation, I was very eager to do so.

A heavy silence followed my somewhat fervent explanation. My arguments did not appear to have convinced him and, after carrying out a further perusal of my papers, he gave a deep sigh and turned me over to the third member of the Board.

This officer, a lean, austere-looking individual, had before him on the table a large maquette showing a river snaking its way down from an inner harbour to the sea. On the river was a bewildering array of shoals, marking buoys of different shapes and colours, and toy models of ships. Pushing towards me a miniature destroyer, I was told that my task was to navigate it from the coast up-river, using all the proper channels, and to bring it safely alongside one of the jetties in the harbour.

Apart from the short course at Portsmouth, my previous seamanship experience was zero, so, swallowing hard, it was with trembling fingers that I set out to fulfil my mission. Half-way up river, my inquisitor abruptly ordered me to stop and, in a voice edged with sarcasm, said, "Do you realize that if you maintain the course you have chosen you will find yourself high and dry in a farmer's field?"

Feeling very embarrassed, I heaved a sigh of relief when, after one or two more questions, I was passed to the one remaining board member who, during my previous ordeal, had been occupied turning over the papers in my file.

Without raising his head he said, "I see that during the past three years you have been serving in the Middle East," and then, addressing me, added, "*Tetekellem bi l'arabi?*" (Can you speak Arabic?).

"*Aiwa, ya sidi*," (Yes, sir), I replied immediately, whereupon he asked several more questions in Arabic, to which I was able to respond without too much difficulty and, apparently, to his satisfaction.

The senior officer of the Board then dismissed me, indicating that I was to exit through a door other than the one I had used to enter the room. Doing so, I found myself alone in a small room, not much larger than a cubicle, with two doors. Feeling dry-mouthed and extremely miserable, I was convinced that I had 'blown it' as I sat there, listening to the low hum of conversation coming from the interview room I had just vacated. I had visions of having to return to Portsmouth Barracks and being drafted to Lord knows where.

After what seemed to be an eternity, an officer came through the other door of the room and I could hardly believe my ears when he announced, "Soars, I'm pleased to have to advise you that you have passed the Selection Board. Report to the office now, where you'll receive all your instructions for joining *King Alfred*."

Almost trance-like, I walked along the corridor to the office. I fully realized that ahead of me lay several weeks of gruelling hard work, with always the grim possibility of not being capable of achieving my goal, but I had just surmounted one tough hurdle and I was now well on my way!

13. Drill, Depth Charges and 'Dipping Daisy'

It was on a bright, sunny morning in early April that, together with several other successful candidates, I was transported the short distance to our new ship, H.M.S. *King Alfred*, which turned out to be an extensive modern building situated on the beach side of the Esplanade in West Hove. Constructed just prior to the outbreak of war, its original purpose was a leisure sports complex, complete with Olympic-size swimming pool, but the Admiralty decided that, subject to certain structural changes, it could become an ideal centre for training the thousands of officers needed in the Royal Naval Volunteer Reserve (the "Wavy Navy" or, as the professional Royal Navy types called them, "the amateur sailors").

On arrival, when I came to check in, there was some brief initial confusion as, being a Petty Officer Writer, it was at first thought that I was the staff replacement they had been expecting, rather than an aspiring cadet for the officers' course. This contretemps was eventually sorted out and I was directed to a classroom, where I found several other ratings already assembled. They were a mixed bag, representing all branches of the service, and some of them appeared much younger than myself. In fact, it passed through my mind that one or two of them were so youthful that, if they were to succeed in passing the course, they would become Midshipmen rather than Sub-Lieutenants.

My reveries were-interrupted when a RNVR Lieutenant briskly entered the room, called us to order and told us to be seated. He then introduced himself.

"My name is G and I will be your Divisional Officer all the time you are here. You, collectively, will be known as the Duncan Division. All the trainee divisions are given the names of famous British admirals. Nelson and Drake, I am sure, are well-known to you all but what do you know about Admiral Duncan?"

Complete silence from the assembled cadets.

As it happened, during my stay in Portsmouth, I had picked up a book recounting famous British naval engagements and, as luck would have it, I remembered reading about Duncan's exploits, so I raised my hand.

"He was in command of the North Sea Squadron when we were at war with France and Holland in the late 18th century. He carried out the successful blockade of Texel, which almost ruined the Dutch shipping trade, and later he scored a brilliant victory at the battle of Camperdown. He also put down the Mutiny of the Nore in the same year. When he was pensioned off he became Viscount Duncan of Camperdown."

"Well done," said Lieutenant G. "You certainly know your naval history." Then, addressing the class he said, "Next item on the agenda. It's normal routine here for one cadet in each division to act as a sort of liaison officer between the Divisional Officer and the class. This person is elected in the democratic way," he added, and then, pointing to myself and two other cadets, said, "You, you and you are hereby nominated as candidates and I call upon you three to give one minute electioneering speeches, after which the class will vote as to whom they want elected."

After our impromptu orations there was a show of hands and I was declared elected. Was it my profound knowledge of naval history that had been instrumental in swinging the vote my way or the fact that I was the senior rating present?

I soon was to discover that this honorary position added a considerable amount of additional chores to what was to be a very busy daily routine. It was my job to ensure that all 49 members of Duncan Division were present and correct for whatever activity was scheduled on the course programme. If anybody happened to be absent during roll-call, I was in trouble if I was unable to give a valid reason for his absence, though I must say that, by and large, I received excellent co-operation from all my fellow cadets.

Before being dismissed, Lieutenant G gave us a brief outline of the many subjects which would be dealt with during the course and also described the daily routine we would be expected to follow. One sobering point to which he made reference was that any cadet failing to reach the high standard required would have his C.W. papers destroyed and would then be sent back to his home depot to resume normal service. Such action would be taken, where necessary, at the end of each week and we were advised to scan the noticeboard in the auditorium each Saturday morning. Those whose names appeared under the Duncan Division heading were "out".

This, I thought to myself, seemed to be a somewhat callous method of dealing with those who did not make the grade, but in retrospect it was, of course, preferable to subjecting a man to the rigours of the entire length of the training period and only then notifying him. As it turned out, our division completed the course with only 36 survivors from the original 49 hopefuls.

After this pep-talk, a staff Chief Petty Officer was introduced and he issued us with distinguishing white cadet cap-bands, khaki gaiters (indicative that there was parade-ground bashing in store) and white armbands, marked from DN1 to DN49 (mine was DN42). He took us to a large dormitory in the basement of the building, where we found beds bearing numbers corresponding to those appearing on the armbands.

The remainder of that first day was spent getting accustomed to the layout of the establishment and mingling with the cadets of other, more advanced in training, divisions, to glean as much information as possible as to what we could expect in the weeks ahead.

We found out that, during the weeks that followed, there did not seem to be enough hours in the day to absorb all the knowledge which was being thrown at us. The life was spartan. The day started at 5.30 a.m. with twenty minutes of physical training on the road behind the establishment, adjacent to the beach. Clad only in singlet and shorts, regardless of the state of the weather, we went through all the required exercises, including, I remember well, several excruciating press-ups which, as the road was gravelly, left us with pieces of grit painfully embedded in the palms of our hands. After that, we would stagger into the showers, hurriedly dress and to breakfast by 7 a.m.

The meals at "K.A." were ample, but the menu monotonous, which was hardly surprising bearing in mind the strict food rationing which prevailed at that time. We were surprised to find that, instead of naval personnel, the catering was in the hands of a civilian firm and we were served at long tables in the immense dining-room by a team of efficient waitresses, some of whom were quite attractive. A "buzz" soon reached our ears, however, that any cadet attempting a liaison with one would find himself "in the rattle" (i.e. placed on a charge). In fact, rumour had it that one particularly pretty girl had become known as "Dipping Daisy" because of the number of cadets who had "dipped" (i.e. failed the course) as the direct result of a dalliance with her!

There may have been an element of truth in this or, on the other hand, it could have been just another of the many items of gossip which circulated amongst the cadets.

It was also alleged to be factual that a staff officer, armed with binoculars, kept a close watch on the main gate where, each morning, a newspaper vendor was allowed to sell his wares – and God help the unwary cadet who purchased one of the more sensational "rags." Again, only a rumour but, nevertheless, it was interesting to see the unusual number of copies of the *Times* or *Daily Telegraph* in the hands of the cadets!

With each day, except Sunday, crammed with an exhausting round of instruction of every conceivable kind, the time passed quickly and I found it amazing how much it is possible to learn in a hurry when you have to!

Many hours were spent delving into the mechanical intricacies of all the weapons of modern warfare, from mines, torpedoes and depth-charges to all the different types of guns – Vickers, Sten, Oerlikon, Lewis, etc – and even the rudiments of chemical warfare.

Then, days would be spent outdoors, transmitting morse code and semaphore messages and memorizing the International Code of Flags and Pennants used in signalling.

Also, half-days were spent afloat in the nearby Portslade Basin, an internal stretch of water near the local gasworks, where each one of us, under the critical eye of a seasoned Chief Petty Officer, got the opportunity to take a turn at the wheel and learn the basics of ship handling.

Long hours were allocated to classroom instruction in the subjects of navigation, chart-reading and battle strategy. Also, we pored over the more important articles in the voluminous naval 'bible' entitled *King's Regulations and Admiralty Instructions*.

Sandwiched between the classroom sessions was daily squad drill on the parade ground, where each one of us would have to take turns in marching the division through complicated manoeuvres, under the discerning eye of our Divisional Officer.

Even after a wearying day of instruction it was not always possible to look forward to an uninterrupted night's sleep, for all cadets were on a roster for sentry duty for one or other of the three night watches. The first watch (8p.m to midnight) was tolerable in that you lost only one or two hours sleep; the middle watch (midnight to 4a.m.) was dreaded; whilst the morning watch (4a.m. to 8 a.m.) was undoubtedly the favourite, as it meant missing P.T. that morning! The sentry duty involved pairs of cadets, armed with loaded rifles and fixed bayonets, patrolling the lengthy perimeter of "KA". Random checks on the sentries' vigilance were made by the Duty Staff Officer who, when challenged, had to give the correct password. Failure to do so could be fatal, as the sentry had strict instructions to open fire if the approaching person did not halt in his tracks.

For those cadets who, despite all the daily activity, still had some energy left, there were inter-divisional cricket matches organised at the nearby Hove Park.

When, on June 6th 1944, the news of the Allied landings in Normandy reached us, there was jubilation amongst the staff and cadets, mixed, however, with regret that we were not taking part in this historical event. Just one week later, a group of us were taking advantage of a brief off-duty period between lessons (by basking in the warm afternoon sun) when we heard the throb of a distant engine. Looking seawards, we saw what appeared to be a miniature plane, streaking towards the coast. It passed over our heads, leaving us to conjecture what it was. We did not have long to wait, for that evening it was announced on the BBC that several jet-propelled flying-bombs had landed in the outskirts of London, causing casualties and extensive damage.

These projectiles were the forerunners of over three thousand of these terror weapons – V1's or *doodlebugs*, as they came to be known by the long-suffering civilian population.

No sooner had our defence forces learned to cope with these destructive devices than the enemy shifted to the even more lethal rocket-propelled V2 which, because of its faster-than-sound speed, gave no indication of its approach until it exploded on impact, causing tremendous devastation.

It was feared that German scientists were on the verge of perfecting atomic warheads for these monstrosities, which would then have the capability of destroying complete cities, but fortunately the Allied advance was able to reach the launch pads before they had time to fulfil this murderous objective.

I was feeling fairly confident of success as we entered the final week of the course but then, on Saturday morning after breakfast, when I, in company with several of my fellow cadets, made our ritual visit to the noticeboard, I recoiled in disbelief when, under the heading of *Duncan Division*, I saw my name!

Falling in later for the usual morning inspection, I was feeling absolutely crestfallen. It must have shown on my face, for when Lieutenant G came abreast of me he paused and, in a low voice, said, "Have you seen the noticeboard?"

Miserably, I nodded my head.

"No need to worry," he murmured. "Make sure you report to the Captain's office by 9.30 a.m."

With that, he continued his progress along the line of cadets.

Despite this reassuring comment, I was still feeling uneasy when I arrived at the Captain's outer office and gave my name to the Third Officer Wren who was sitting there. She asked me to wait and disappeared into an adjoining room for what seemed to be an eternity as I sat there with my thoughts in a turmoil. Eventually she returned and I was ushered into the hallowed presence of Captain J.N. Pelly RN, who was flanked by two of his officers.

Smiling pleasantly, he said, "No doubt you're wondering why you've been summoned here?"

Dry-mouthed, I managed to answer, "Yes sir."

He continued. "It's to offer you my personal congratulations, Soars, as you have completed the course as the top cadet in your division." He and the other two officers then shook my hand and wished me well in all my future endeavours.

Feeling quite exhilarated, I rejoined the division, where further felicitations were forthcoming as, in my absence, everyone had been advised of their promotions by Lieutenant G, who had, at the same time, explained the reason for my unexpected visit to the Captain's office.

Following the midday meal, several of us made a quick dash across the seafront to Gieves (one of many naval outfitting firms which had, with obvious foresight, leased properties in close proximity to K.A.). We gave instructions for them to proceed with our new suits, the measurements for which their tailors had taken earlier in the course.

Then a telegram to Alexandria, Egypt, to inform Nahidé of the good news…

The few remaining days were fully occupied attending to the myriad matters involved in the transition from the lower to the upper deck, including a fond farewell to my kitbag and hammock – my constant travelling companions for more than three years.

Finally, the passing out ceremony, the group photographs and the farewell dinner, at which we all expressed the hope to meet again some day, somewhere. As it transpired, of the

34 successful cadets, only three were destined to cross my path later, but one of these became a very close friend and, eventually, the godfather of one of my daughters.

I have often wondered if all the others were fortunate enough to survive until the end of the hostilities and were not numbered amongst those far too many "King Alfreds" who "did not make it".

This is to Certify

that

THOMAS HENRY SOARS

P.O.Wtr:(Ty)   D/MX 63523

(Name, Rating and Official No.)

after completing the preliminary period of his training in H.M.S. KING ALFRED as a SPECIALLY SELECTED RATING has been promoted to the rank of

TEMP. { *ACTING SUB.-LIEUTENANT* / ~~SUB.-LIEUTENANT~~ / ~~MIDSHIPMAN~~ } R.N.V.R.

_____   _____
Training Commander   Instructor Commander

Approved.

23rd June, 1944.   Captain

Promotion certificate, awarded on completion of officers' course.

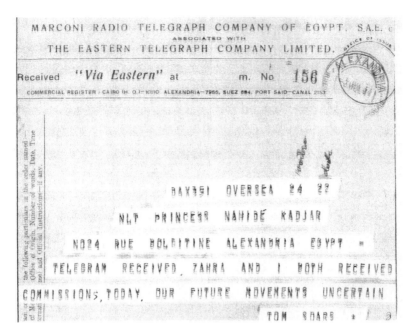

Marconi telegraph, sent by author to his fiancée on successful completion of course (Zahra was a mutual friend from Alexandria, Egypt also on the same course)

14. Back to the Med

Upon completion of my metamorphosis from messdeck to wardroom, I bade a fond farewell to HMS *King Alfred* and, after a short but very welcome spell of home leave, I was given a temporary appointment to the Royal Naval Barracks at Chatham.

Once I had settled in, I decided to put into operation my plan to return to the Mediterranean or, better still, Alexandria, and I lost no time in making my wishes clear to one of the Paymasters employed in the Captain's Office. My initial approach was greeted with incredulity. "You have a fat chance of getting back there, old boy, but I'll bear you in mind and we'll see what comes up."

After this conversation, my days became fully occupied with my new job – that of training new entry ratings – so much so that I had almost forgotten about it when, one morning in mid-July, I was summoned to the Captain's Office, where a Wren clerk handed me a flimsy slip of paper. To the Wren's astonishment, I whooped for joy when I read: *Acting Sub. Lieut. T.H. Soars is hereby appointed to N.O.I.C. Naples, for disposal.*

The phrase "for disposal" was somewhat disconcerting, but I was thrilled to realize that, so soon, I had been presented with an opportunity to get back to the Med, even though Naples was over a thousand miles from my desired ultimate destination.

Before the week ended I was on my way to Liverpool, to board a transport which was carrying officers and ratings of all three services and, to my surprise, a small contingent of returning ex-prisoners of war who, since Italy's unconditional surrender last autumn, were now our allies. Considering that, for three years, we had been slaughtering each other in North and East Africa and the Med, it was quite extraordinary to witness the camaraderie on board between victor and vanquished.

I attended lessons given daily by a young Italian naval officer, which gave me a useful rudimentary grasp of the Italian language, which was to be of assistance later after reaching our destination.

Unescorted, we travelled at a fast pace across the Bay of Biscay, but instead of putting into port at Gibraltar, as had been anticipated, we sailed through the Straits non-stop to Italy.

"See Naples and die." This oft-repeated expression had been on my mind that morning whilst shaving, as we neared our destination. I pondered on the double meaning this phrase now conjured up. How many individuals, both allied and enemy, had so recently met their ends during the fierce fighting in this theatre of war? Dressing quickly, I rushed up on deck to take in the vista which presented itself off the starboard bow.

It was a picture long to be remembered; the wide sweep of the coast embracing the Bay of Naples, with the city superbly situated in the northern corner and sprawling over the surrounding hills, with the still active Vesuvius providing an ominous backdrop on this clear morning in early August.

As the ship entered the harbour, the soft, idyllic scene gradually became hardened by reality as we surveyed the tremendous devastation – the combined result of recent Allied bombing and enemy demolition of buildings and facilities prior to their evacuation of the city. Instead of mooring up to a jetty, we came alongside the broad bottom of a vessel which, presumably bombed, had turned completely upside down. We disembarked on this and then across wooden gangways to the jetty proper.

Shortly after arriving, two lorries arrived to take the naval personnel to the base, located in an old fort, facing the harbour. Checking in with the Officer of the Watch, I was directed to onshore accommodation and ordered to report the following morning. A station-wagon was provided to transport two other Sub-Lieutenants and myself into the city, which seemed to be remarkably devoid of traffic.

Turning off the main Via Roma onto a side-street, we came to a standstill outside an unimpressive *pension*, where we were deposited with our baggage. Immediately, a pleasant-faced young Italian emerged to greet us, grabbed our suitcases and escorted us into the building. An elderly man in a shabby uniform received us in the lobby and requested us to enter our names in a tattered guest-book, which, I noticed, already contained the names of other naval officers of junior rank. Later, I learned that this was one of several hotels and boarding houses which had been requisitioned by the occupying allied forces.

The accommodation was clean, the meals reasonably well prepared and the service very attentive. We soon discovered that the hotel staff who waited on us had only recently looked after German naval personnel, and there was ample evidence of their prior occupation in the form of German magazines, books and even one or two family photographs. Their leave-taking must have been very hasty!

Reporting for duty the following morning, I was advised that I would be required for watch-keeping duties at the base, pending a more permanent appointment, but I soon found out that these duties were not unduly onerous. In fact, during the five weeks I was in Naples as a supernumerary to the normal complement, I found that I had a considerable amount of spare time on my hands.

I made the maximum use of this windfall by exploring the surrounding region of Campania, which contained such renowned beauty spots as Sorrento, Pozzuoli, Positano (where steep flights of stone steps serve as streets in this cliff-hanging town), Amalfi, which, I was interested to discover, was, in the Middle Ages, a maritime city-state rivalling Genoa and Venice. The scenic islands of Capri and Ischia I reached by courtesy of a friend stationed in the torpedo boat base at Castellammare.

During my stay, Vesuvius smiled down serenely, with just a vestige of fumes above its crater and, only after visiting the archaeological sites at Pompeii and Herculaneum, both once thriving cities which, in the year 79 AD, were completely buried in volcanic ash, was I able to fully comprehend the power of the sleeping giant's fury.

A few miles south, I surveyed the evidence of more recent devastation and this by the hands of man, at Salerno, where the first large-scale Allied landing on Italy's mainland had taken place almost exactly a year ago. On the day I went to Salerno I was fortunate enough to meet three American soldiers who offered me a lift back into Naples. They had an open jeep (a vehicle quite new to me) and, as the driver turned onto the main *autostrade*, he cautioned me to hold tight. Once on this super-modern highway, the jeep took off like a bat out of hell and it was with no little relief that, after thirty miles in about fifteen minutes, we reduced speed as we entered the southern outskirts of the city.

Here, another new experience awaited me. The driver said, "I'm parched, do you guys feel like a coke?" His companions agreed readily and, not wanting to appear unsociable, but not exactly aware of what was being offered, I also nodded my head.

Only after we turned into the forecourt of a large brick factory building, bearing a glossy red and white sign, did I realize that I had been invited for my first taste of that great American beverage, Coca-Cola! Entering the building, I was astonished to find hundreds of bottles rattling merrily along a seemingly interminable assembly line. The corporal who had greeted my companions on our arrival deftly whisked four full bottles off as they went past and handed them to us. It was an extremely welcome and refreshing drink on a day when the mercury was hovering around 85 degrees Fahrenheit and my nerves were somewhat shattered after our hair-raising trip from Salerno!

I learned that the establishment of this bottling plant had been one of the first priorities after the Americans had entered Naples and supplies of the necessary machinery and concentrate had been shipped from the USA.

These days of tourist-like leisure were destined not to last and one morning in early September I was called to the Captain's Office.

"We've found you an appointment," the rosy-faced Paymaster Lieutenant announced, and handed me a slip of paper, which instructed me to join His Hellenic Majesty's Ship *Kanaris* as the B.N.L.O. (British Naval Liaison Officer).

"But I don't speak any Greek," I protested.

"That shouldn't be a problem," replied the Paymaster cheerfully. "You are French-speaking and we are told that the Captain of *Kanaris* has a smattering of both English and French.

Resignedly, I asked, "Where do I join her?"

To my surprise, he answered "Bari, about one hundred and fifty miles distant on the Adriatic coast," and added, "we'll fix you up with transportation."

I packed my belongings and by early afternoon was well on my way, in a 15cwt Dodge, driven by a young Maltese seaman.

Arriving at Bari, I reported to the N.O.I.C. and was annoyed to be advised that the *Kanaris* had left during the night, destination Alexandria – exactly where I wanted to go!

"Don't worry, old boy, we'll get you there somehow," said the N.O.I.C., shuffling through some papers on his desk. Finally, he shook his head. "I'm afraid there's nothing due to leave Bari in that direction, but there *is* a Dutch freighter down at Brindisi which is scheduled to sail for Alex tomorrow evening."

"Where's Brindisi?" I enquired, wearily.

"It's about seventy miles down the coast, south of here. I'll have my driver take you there first thing tomorrow morning and I'll send them a signal tonight to say that you are coming."

I enjoyed a good supper at the base, during which, in conversation with other officers, I managed to find out exactly what the duties of a B.N.L.O. consisted of. Apparently, most of our destroyer flotillas included one or more ships belonging to allied navies and these always carried a British officer, whose job it was to handle and interpret signals whilst at sea and to act as liaison when dealing with victualling and pay arrangements when in port.

The *Kanaris*, I was told, had already established a reputation as a 'fighting ship' and last year had played a prominent part in supporting the various Allied landings on the coasts of Sicily.

The following morning, after an early breakfast, I was on my way to Brindisi and, during the journey, had time to reflect upon my good fortune. Whilst in Naples, several of my brother officers had been posted to ships which were being prepared for the invasion of southern France, the strategic plans for which were being directed from the Allied H.Q. at Caserta, near to Naples, and here was I, getting ready to go in the opposite direction!

On arrival at the docks in Brindisi, I found the Dutch freighter was already preparing to sail (earlier than I had been informed) and by early afternoon we were well out in the Strait of Otranto. As I paced the deck, breathing in the refreshing sea breeze, I thought to myself that, here I was, about to accomplish what the prophets of doom back in England had said was impossible, namely to return to exactly the same place I had left last year.

I pushed to the back of my mind the very strong possibility that after joining *Kanaris* my stay in Alexandria could well turn out to be of limited duration.

15. Once Again in Alex

The voyage to Alexandria was uneventful and, on the day of our arrival, Sunday 10th September 1944, gradually, through the early morning haze, I was able to discern the familiar outline of the Ras-el-Tin promontory, with its graceful lighthouse, still clothed in wartime camouflage, covering its normal black and white stripes.

We entered the harbour – one of the most beautiful in the world – and moored up to a jetty. After thanking the captain and crew for their hospitality, I disembarked and hailed one of the horse-drawn *gharries* waiting there and directed the driver to take me to the nearby naval base, HMS *Nile* – where I knew I would be able to obtain directions for locating the *Kanaris*.

"She entered dry dock yesterday for some repairs," I was informed by the Officer on duty, "and there's just a skeleton crew on board. Everyone else has taken advantage of a few days shore leave."

Alexandria had a very large Greek population and I had no doubt that most of the crew would have relatives or friends eager to receive them.

"We can fix you up with a billet here," offered the O.O.D. "or, if you prefer, you can go ashore, as long as you let us know where we can contact you at short notice. Also, I'd suggest that you phone this office daily at, say, 0800 hours, to enquire whether *Kanaris* is ready to go to sea."

I thanked him for his offer of accommodation, explaining that, having recently spent three years in Alex, I was familiar with the city and had in mind going directly to the Union Club, where I hoped to obtain a room.

There being no naval transport scheduled to leave for downtown until midday and wanting to make the most of the precious time available to me, I decided to take one of the taxis waiting on the rank outside the main gate of the base.

As we sped along the wide Corniche road towards the city centre I felt a distinct sense of being back home as we passed the many landmarks familiar to me, and my mind strayed to the stirring events that had occurred during my previous sojourn in these surroundings. Suddenly conscious that the taxi had come to a standstill, having reached the club, I snapped out of my reverie, paid off the driver and, with the help of the doorman carrying my baggage, went inside to the reception desk.

It had been too early to telephone Nahidé from the harbour but, having checked in, I lost no time in doing so. She was astounded to hear my voice and overjoyed to learn that I was actually in Alexandria. She had been aware from letters I had written her after arriving in Italy that I was back in the Med, but my very sudden departure from Naples had prevented further communication.

We arranged to meet at midday at Baudrot's for lunch. I had already arrived at the restaurant when she walked in, looking radiant, and it was wonderful to hold her in my arms again after an absence of almost nine months.

Happily, she related various items of news concerning her family and friends that had occurred during my absence and I was content to let her chatter away, for this delayed my having to impart the sad fact that my stay ashore could well be a very short one. Eventually, however, as gently as possible, I made her aware of the *Kanaris* appointment, at which point she became crestfallen to the state of tears.

I endeavoured to comfort her by pointing out that my ship formed part of a flotilla based in Alex, which meant that I could expect to be back in port from time to time. This attempt at reassurance did little to revive her good spirits but, after a while, she managed a brave smile and took my hand saying, "It's really a miracle that you managed to return at all, so let us thank God and make the most of whatever time we may have before you have to return to the ship." She then added, "I hope it takes a long time to repair your ship!"

During the following three days we spent every minute together, re-visiting old haunts and fitting in dutiful calls on family and old friends, all of whom were surprised to see me again and congratulated me on my new status. The weather was perfect and we spent a lot of time on the beach at Stanley Bay, swimming and picnicking, strolling around the picturesque Nouzha Gardens where, two years previously, we had danced together at the Swiss charity soirée and even going to the 'Royal' to see the movie *Gone with the Wind*, but always, at the back of my mind, the nagging thought that, any day now, I would be recalled to join my ship.

Then, during the night of the fourth day, along came my *deus ex machina*! At around two o'clock in the morning I awakened, as sick as a dog, and spent the remainder of the night in the bathroom. I was sharing the room with a young R.A.F. officer who, as my condition had so deteriorated by the dawn, insisted, despite my protests, on calling a medical officer, who happened to be staying at the club. He found that I was running a high fever and, as a result of vomiting and diarrhoea, was fast becoming dehydrated.

"It looks as though you've got food-poisoning or enteritis," he announced, "and the quicker we get you into a hospital the better."

After that, I vaguely remember being rolled onto a stretcher and, with my personal effects balanced on top of me, being carried out to an ambulance, where I fell into a sleep of exhaustion.

I awakened to find myself in a large high-ceilinged room with four beds, all occupied. My bed was facing a window, which looked out onto a splendid garden, full of trees and flowers.

A nurse came in and gave me a dose of a disagreeable-tasting liquid (I later discovered that it was a drug called *emetine*, derived from the *ipecacuanha* plant). She advised me that I was in the Naval Officers' Hospital at San Stefano. Before the war this attractive building had been a hotel and casino.

I later discovered that the Union Club had notified HMS *Nile* regarding my predicament and they had dispatched the ambulance to transport me to this hospital.

I spent the next two weeks there, under close observation, for apparently I was on the verge of dysentery, so each morning I had to field Matron's imperious enquiry, "Any blood today?"

With the aid of a special milk and beef-tea diet and daily afternoon visits from a very concerned Nahidé, my condition gradually improved, but I had lost some weight and was still feeling quite weak when, on 29th September, the attending physician pronounced me fit enough to return to duty the following day.

Nahidé made her usual visit later that day and was most depressed to learn the latest news and to realize that our all-too-brief encounter had come to an end. With a heavy heart, I bade her farewell, not knowing when – or even *if* – we would meet again.

I had an almost sleepless night and it was with a certain foreboding that I boarded the station-wagon that had been arranged to take me to HMS *Nile* at Ras-el-Tin. Arriving there, I staggered into the O.O.D.'s office and, weak from carrying my luggage, slumped down into the nearest chair.

The O.O.D. glanced at me and enquired "What can I do for you?"

"I've just been discharged from hospital," I replied wearily, "and I have to join the *Kanaris*."

He looked at some papers on his desk and then made an announcement which was like music to my ears.

"That destroyer put to sea about a week ago. We phoned the Club in town and were told that you'd gone into hospital so, at short notice, we had to obtain another Subby to replace you."

He must have mistaken the stunned look on my face as disappointment, for he added, " Very sorry about that, old chap."

"What happens to me now then?" I asked.

"Just give me a minute whilst I make a phone call," he replied. He picked up the phone and, with the noise of the typewriter in the background, I could not pick up the gist of his conversation. He finally replaced the phone and said, "They can do with an extra hand at *Sphinx*, so we're sending you up there, on a temporary basis, until we can find you a more permanent job."

So, later that day, still finding it hard to believe, I was once again on my way eastwards along the corniche road, passing en route the hospital I had left just hours before, finally arriving at the naval shore establishment known as HMS *Sphinx*.

The First Lieutenant, a Lieutenant Commander RNVR, gave me a cordial welcome, asked about my previous experience and then spent some time explaining the *raison d'être* of *Sphinx*, finishing up with a brief outline of what my duties would be. I listened as attentively as I could, but only with difficulty could I keep my eyes open, so it was with considerable relief when the First Lieutenant paused and said, "They phoned me from *Nile*, explaining that you came out of hospital this morning. You seem to be all-in, so you'd better get a meal and then have an early night. Report to me at 0800 hours tomorrow."

I thanked him and, with the help of the Chief Steward, found the cabin to which I had been allocated.

There now remained one item of paramount importance which I had to attend to. I telephoned Nahidé.

"I'm still here," I said.

"What's happened?" she enquired anxiously.

I went over the surprising turn of events since we had parted company the previous evening and she was overjoyed – so much so that I did not have the heart to point out that this latest development would only be of a temporary nature also.

"Let's take things one at a time," I said to myself, as I put the phone down and returned to my cabin.

As it happened, my run of good luck was to continue. About a week later, as I came into the mess for breakfast after my first twenty-four hour watch as O.O.D., the First Lieutenant handed me a copy of a signal which read:

> *To C.O. Sphinx from C-in-C Levant. Copy to C.O. Nile.*
> *To replace Lieut. C being discharged U.K. confirm you may retain Sub. Lt. Soars for your permanent staff.*

The No.1 looked at me and said, "Any objections?"

"None whatsoever, Sir!" I replied.

I could have kissed him!

16. A Ship in the Desert

The famous Corniche road in Alexandria stretches from the promontory of Ras-el-Tin as far east as the summer palace of Montazeh – a distance of about twenty-five kilometres – and, close to the eastern end, is the suburb of Sidi Bishr where, opposite the beach, were several acres of sprawling sand dunes. It was in this somewhat unusual location that, in September 1940, their Lordships at the Admiralty, in their wisdom, decided that the shore base to be known as HMS *Sphinx* was commissioned.

Sphinx was run exactly like a ship. Its complement divided into port and starboard watches, followed a strict naval daily routine and, when the crew went 'ashore' – that is, into the city – they travelled in *liberty boats* – only these happened to be lorries.

Unlike many other naval vessels, its activities never made news headlines, (except on one memorable occasion we heard about, when an over-enthusiastic announcer on Berlin radio, in giving the names of allied vessels sunk or damaged, had included HMS *Sphinx!*) However, during the entire war years, it fulfilled a very useful purpose as the main naval distribution centre in the Eastern Mediterranean and Suez Canal area.

Contingents of naval ratings and Royal Marines would arrive periodically from the United Kingdom – usually by troop transport – and would be housed temporarily in *Sphinx* whilst awaiting to be drafted to various ships in the fleet. The personnel they replaced would arrive in *Sphinx*, where they would be held until suitable transport became available for their passage back to their home ports.

Dealing with this continual fluctuation of numbers required a lot of careful organization. At times the camp would be almost empty, apart from the permanent staff, but then suddenly build up to as many as fifteen hundred or even more, before we were able to move them out to their destinations.

The permanent ship's company numbered about one hundred ratings and from twelve to fourteen officers, which included the Captain, First Lieutenant, two Paymasters, three Medical Officers, a Chaplain and four or five executive branch watch-keeping officers, of which I was one. Apart from their watch-keeping duties, these officers all had specific duties which collectively ensured the smooth running of *Sphinx*.

I was put in charge of 'ship's boats', which meant that I had the responsibility of supervising the care, maintenance and scheduling of a fleet of sixteen lorries, three cars and two motorcycles, all of which were in constant daily use for transporting ratings, with their kitbags and hammocks, to and from ships in the harbour, or on shore leave, or for bringing in supplies which could consist of anything from sugar to cement.

My other duties were Baggage and Mail Officer and, for good measure, Education Officer, which involved holding regular weekly information classes for those hostilities-only ratings who wished to prepare themselves in readiness for their eventual return to civilian life.

During the four years prior to my arrival that *Sphinx* had been in existence, an incredible amount of hard work had been carried out to transform the original empty, barren location into an efficient, well-planned naval establishment, complete with all the necessary accommodation and administrative buildings. A large area had been levelled off to form a parade-ground, which was also used for football and cricket matches, organised on several evenings each week and at weekends.

Located in other parts of the camp were tennis courts, a rifle and small arms range, a gymnasium, a splendid church, a hospital, a huge cinema and a large, well-equipped garage and workshop. All these buildings were interconnected by a first-class system of paths and roadways, many of which were lined with well-tended gardens. Beyond this central core of buildings there were neat lines of approximately three hundred tents, many with concrete bases and each capable of sleeping four ratings.

Much of the construction work had been done by voluntary labour. As a routine we would enquire of each batch of new arrivals whether any of them, in pre-war days, had been employed in trades such as bricklayers, plasterers, joiners, electricians or plumbers, and, if so, whether they would be prepared to lend a hand on various on-going projects whilst awaiting onward passage to their final destinations. We always obtained more volunteers than were actually needed which, undoubtedly, was because the alternative employment of cleaning ship, assisting in the galleys and mess-halls and sentry and guard duties, were less attractive pastimes!

After the cessation of hostilities, the days of HMS *Sphinx* were numbered and, in the summer of 1946, the white ensign was lowered for the last time and the entire base handed over to the Egyptian Army.

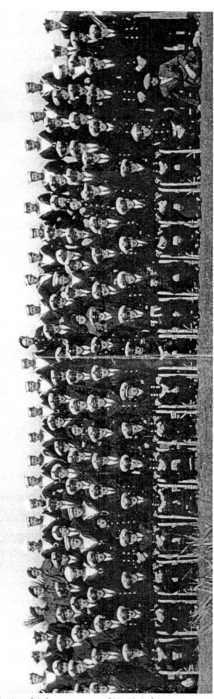

Entire ship's company of HMS *Sphinx*, 1944.

Main entrance to HMS *Sphinx*.

Close-up of concrete statue at camp entrance.

An aerial view of the camp at HMS *Sphinx*.

Dedication of the new chapel at HMS *Sphinx* by Bishop of Egypt.

Author with transport division ratings, HMS *Sphinx*.

Sunday morning divisions at HMS *Sphinx*.

17. Trials and Tribulations of an O.O.D.

Being the Officer of the Watch or, more correctly for a shore base, the Officer of the Day, meant occupying an office in the Administration Building – which was located just inside the main entrance in *Sphinx* – from 8 a.m. to 8 a.m. the following morning, being relieved only for one hour at midday and in the evening, for meals. During this 24-hour vigil, everything that occurred in and around the camp became your responsibility

   If fortunate, you might be able to get a night's sleep on the bunk in the small cabin adjacent to the office, after the last 'liberty boat', arriving from the city at around midnight, had disgorged its usual cargo of boisterous passengers. Frequently, you would be awakened, at any time during the night, to answer a telephone call from a shore patrol of any one of the three services, reporting that a rating from *Sphinx* had been causing a disturbance in one way or another and requesting an escort to be sent into the city to collect the delinquent.

   This would entail arousing the duty Regulating Petty Officer (RPO), who would arrange for our duty patrol, consisting of a Leading Seaman and two Able Seamen, all armed, to be transported into Alexandria. Two or three hours later they would return, usually with a very intoxicated and obstreperous rating in tow. He would be confined, often with considerable difficulty, in one of the cells located along the corridor from the office, in order to 'cool off' until the following morning when, hopefully, he would be sober enough to be formally charged. Before incarceration, however, one had to be certain that a man's condition was due to excess alcohol and not as a result of any medical cause which, if suspected, required contacting the duty Medical Officer for procedural advice.

During officer training at *King Alfred* it had been instilled into us that, in dealing with defaulters, it was essential to "maintain a dignified calm at all times", but on one occasion I remember well, I had the utmost difficulty in complying with this wise counsel.

Late one night, the shore patrol had brought in a young Able Seaman who had been apprehended in an out-of-bounds brothel in a sleazy section of the old city. All ratings going on shore leave received very strict instructions, for obvious reasons, to avoid unsupervised brothels in favour of several medically-checked locations which were available in one clearly-defined district.

After the R.P.O. had reported the case to me I ordered the accused to be brought in for investigation. He had a dishevelled and hang-dog appearance and looked decidedly uncomfortable as he faced me across the desk. The Leading Seaman of the shore patrol was there to give evidence and, in readiness, he had written all the details in a small notebook. At my request, he read these out in a monotone voice.

"With Able Seamen A and B I was patrolling in the prescribed downtown area when we were approached by a native boy who informed us that he had seen a sailor entering a house in a street in the out-of-bounds area. I thereupon proceeded with caution to the house in question and, finding the entrance door half-open, I walked inside. In the corridor I heard a noise coming from one of the rooms. I went to the room, opened the door, and there on the floor was Able Seaman X (indicating the accused), lying on top of a native woman."

He paused, cleared his throat, and went on.

"I went up to Able Seaman X and requested to see his Pay and Identity Card."

At this point it was only with the utmost difficulty that I managed to keep a straight face. I could visualize the scene and could imagine the feelings of the poor fellow in front of me being asked to prove his identity in such embarrassing circumstances!

Thanking the Leading Seaman for his report, I addressed the accused, pointing out that he was facing a very serious charge and asking whether he had anything he wished to say. He cast a surly sidelong glance at the Leading Seaman and growled, "Yes, I wish he'd come in just five minutes later!"

I ordered his name to be added to the Defaulter's List, to be placed before the Captain later in the day.

On another occasion, I was informed by the R.P.O. that he had a rating who wished to speak to me regarding a 'personal matter'.

"Any idea what it's about?" I enquired.

"Apparently he's received a telegram, Sir, and thinks he has grounds for compassionate leave."

"Alright, send him in."

He was a smartly turned out Leading Telegraphist in his late twenties who, judging from the look on his face, appeared to have a problem.

"What can I do for you?" I asked.

"Well Sir, it's about this telegram from my mother." He handed me a crumpled piece of paper.

The telegram read: "Betty has baby boy, letter follows, Mum."

"Presumably Betty is your wife. Congratulations, that's a good bit of news."

"It isn't, Sir," replied the rating, tersely. "I've been out here for almost two years!"

I had really put my foot in it and attempted to commiserate with him, as he seemed to be on the verge of tears.

"I can well understand your wish for compassionate leave," I began, "but under existing orders we'll have to have local enquiries made where you live before your request can be approved."

Although this particular case had the appearance of being quite genuine, one had to exercise caution, as there had been previous instances of false information being supplied in an attempt to enable a rating to obtain home leave before he was due for it.

This rating was drafted to a destroyer two days later and I never did get to know the outcome of his request.

In addition to seeing defaulters and requestmen, manifold were the O.O.D.'s duties. Of high importance on the long list was the daily 'tot' issue – a *tot* being one eighth of a pint of rum. Chiefs and Petty officers were allowed to have their allowance supplied neat in their mess-hall, whilst leading hands and below had to line up to consume their *tots*, which were always diluted with an equal part of water.

When "up spirits" was piped, prior to the midday meal, the O.O.D.'s job was to verify that the amount of rum drawn from the cask in the victualling store complied with the daily record of the number of ratings who were entitled to the ration. Sometimes, for one reason or another, there would be an amount left over and, being diluted, this could not be returned to the cask, so it had to be disposed of. Under the officer's supervision, it would be emptied down a drain outside the mess-hall.

One day it came to light that a group of enterprising ratings had been engaged in a thriving trade with this surplus mixture. Ingeniously, they had removed the grill leading to the drain, placed a bucket inside and thus collected the surplus whenever, at the end of the "up spirits" session, it was poured away as ordered by the officer!

At mealtimes it was the O.O.D.'s duty to make a sortie into the mess-halls, pausing at each table to enquire whether anyone had complaints to make about the food. Sometimes this involved tasting some of the food to assess its palatability!

At unannounced times during the day, random inspections of living quarters, kitchens and latrines would be undertaken, occasionally accompanied by the Captain or the First Lieutenant, and invariably a long list of infringements would be noted for subsequent discussion with the offending parties!

The most important event of the day for those ratings who were in the off-duty watch was the striking of *eight bells* at 4pm, which meant that the first of five 'liberty boats' would be leaving for the city. At this time, and at half-hourly intervals thereafter until 6pm, there would be a rush to line up ready for inspection by the O.O.D. before being allowed to board the lorries.

Often, as I walked along the lines to ensure that all these shore-going personnel were correctly and cleanly dressed, my mind would go back to my own early training days as a new entry in 1940, at Trevol, in Cornwall, where our Instructor Officer was an elderly Commissioned Bosun – a World War I veteran recalled out of retirement. He had a pronounced lisp and, when addressing us, his "son" came out as "thun".

The conditions at Trevol were very spartan and we had to wash all our own clothing on "make and mend" days. To reduce the time spent on this unwelcome task, we new entries were inclined to cut corners. The standard shirt issue (for ratings in "fore and aft rig") was white, with detachable collars, which were secured with front and back studs. We soon discovered that the laundry chore became much easier if we simply washed the collars but wore the shirt as long possible. When the jacket was buttoned up, the lapels and the black tie more or less concealed the grimy front of the shirt underneath and, to make doubly sure, one could always hunch one's shoulders!

However, lining-up to go on shore leave into Plymouth one day, my ruse was finally unveiled. As our Commissioned Bosun reached me he paused and said, "Pull back your shoulders, thun." When I did so, he leaned forward to peer closely at my chest and, in a very taunting tone, loud enough for all to hear, announced, "Do you know, thun, this is the first time that I've seen a naval rating wearing a white collar with a khaki shirt!"

Ordered to fall out, I was sent to find a clean shirt (which I was fortunate enough to borrow from a friend) and then reported back to the Commissioned Bosun, who gave me a lengthy lecture on the subject of "cleanliness being next to Godliness" before, to my relief, allowing me to proceed ashore on the next liberty boat!

Perhaps the most arduous chore during the 24-hour watch was the nightly inspection of the camp's perimeter to make sure that there had been no break-ins. This involved tramping around the inside of the thick barbed-wire fence – a distance of approximately one mile – although it always seemed longer than this because of the difficulty of having to trudge through loose sand.

These nocturnal rounds (the times for which were always staggered) were necessary as, in the past, there had been a considerable amount of theft of personal effects, in particular blankets, which, when sold in the native bazaars, could fetch a handsome price.

The O.O.D., armed with a revolver and torch, would be accompanied by three guards, similarly equipped, and, for added weight, I would often take my dog 'Salvage' along for the walk.

The incidence of these thefts had, in recent years, been considerably reduced by the widening and strengthening of the barrier, but there were still some determined individuals who, equipped with wire-cutters, were willing to take the risk of breaking in and, from time to time, we experienced skirmishes. These usually terminated with the arrest of the miscreants, who we would hand over to the local police, from whom, we were told, they could expect really harsh treatment.

18. Requesting Permission to Marry

Having been blessed with the amazing good fortune to land, against all odds, a permanent posting back in Alexandria, Nahidé and I lost no time in giving serious thought to marriage. Both of us were determined not to let this heaven-sent opportunity pass us by, but there were, of course, certain obstacles to be overcome.

First and foremost, there was the question of obtaining the acquiescence of Nahidé's parents to our union and, towards achieving this end, Nahidé wisely enlisted the support of her Swiss friends, but in particular Leonard and Marianne B and Paul and Lilli R. These two families had, in the past, ably demonstrated the influence they enjoyed with Prince Kadjar and his Swiss-born wife.

To our relief, their intervention soon bore fruit, for by mid-October, through the intermediary of Paul R, I was invited to meet the Prince at an exclusive club in down-town Alexandria, with a view to having *'une discussion serieuse'* over morning coffee.

Arriving early at the rendezvous, I was shown into the lounge, where I selected a table in a secluded corner, but from which vantage point I would be able to see the Prince as soon as he entered. After a short interval a very distinguished-looking gentleman entered and gazed around the room. He was a man of medium build, clean-shaven except for a thin, military-style moustache and, in my estimation, probably in his early sixties. He was neatly attired in European-style clothing, but wearing a maroon *tarboosh* and, under one arm, he carried a thin malacca cane.

I sensed immediately that this imposing personage was my fiancée's father and, if all went well, my future father-in-law. As I happened to be the only person present clad in naval uniform, he directly made his way towards me and I, somewhat apprehensively, not being too sure of the protocol involved, rose to meet him, before he reached the table.

He quickly put me at ease by shaking hands in a very cordial manner and, taking his place at the table, summoned a hovering waiter and ordered coffee. After subjecting me to close scrutiny, he took out a slim silver cigarette case and offered me a Turkish cigarette, which I accepted. Over our coffee, he bombarded me, in excellent French, with a variety of questions, mainly about my background, and it was obvious from some of his enquiries that he had already found out quite a lot about me from Paul R.

Thankfully, by the time we had finished our second coffee, I knew that I had passed his interrogation with flying colours, for he shook me by the hand and assured me that he would have no objection to my marrying the youngest of his three daughters. He also indicated that Nahidé, despite her young years, was a very determined individual who had always shown good sense in anything she had undertaken and, in the circumstances, he felt confident that she would make a success of her marriage.

Both Nahidé and I were delighted to hear the result of this interview. Another obstacle had been overcome and now it remained a matter of seeing whether the Royal Navy would raise any objections!

The following day I appeared before my Commanding Officer requesting 'permission to marry' and presented him with full details of my 'intended'.

I found his first reaction rather discouraging.

"This is all very sudden," he said, shaking his head in disbelief. "You've only been here about three weeks!"

Fortunately, I had carefully rehearsed my case and, patiently, I explained that I had been engaged to the lady in question for more than eighteen months, having become acquainted with her during my previous three years in Alexandria when I was on the staff of the B.A.O. I added, for good measure, that she had been introduced to me by a very reputable Swiss subject, who represented, in Egypt, the British insurance company by whom I had been employed pre-war.

To my relief, all this seemed to satisfy my C.O. for he said, "I now understand the situation but, quite frankly, my first thought was that you had become '*non compus mentis*'. We will, of course, have to make certain enquiries, which are routine in wartime, but I cannot foresee any problems. It's getting to be quite an epidemic around here, you're the second of my officers who has decided to marry a local girl."

That evening I told Nahidé of the result of this discussion. She was delighted and, from that time on, it was a matter of "full steam ahead" making preparations for the great day.

Nahidé's very close Swiss friend, Mme B and her two daughters had already volunteered as a kind of 'steering committee' to arrange all the pre-nuptial requirements. Into the fervour of all their organizing I deemed it wise to point out that my C.O. had not yet given me definite permission to marry but had only stated that he "couldn't foresee any difficulties".

"Why would he say that?" Nahidé rather testily enquired.

"A necessary precaution, my dear, in time of war," I replied. "They have to make sure that you're not another Mata Hari!"

My cautionary utterance was brushed to one side in the excitement, as all those involved worked out the details of the upcoming event, for which even the date – Saturday 2nd December – had been arranged.

It was a close call, in that it was not until the last week of November that my anxiety was alleviated when I was handed a copy of a letter which read as follows:

SUBJECT: Sub-Lieutenant T.H. Soars. R.N.V.R.
FROM: Commanding Officer, H.M.S. "Sphinx".
TO: H.B.M. Consul General, Alexandria, Egypt.

This is to certify that the above-named officer has my full permission to marry Princess Nahidé Kadjar

SIGNED: COMMANDER-in-COMMAND

Passing by the entrance to the naval base on the morning of our wedding, I was surprised to see that a large garland of flowers had been hoisted on the yard-arm, next to the white ensign, thus observing true naval tradition announcing that a member of the ship's company was entering matrimony on that day.

Accompanied by two close friends, who had volunteered as witnesses, Nahidé and I appeared before the British Consul General in the morning to undergo the first of two services in one day – the compulsory civic one, to be followed later in the day by a traditional church wedding.

After the consulate session, which was quite brief, we parted company, Nahidé to return to her home to have lunch with her family, leaving me to go back to HMS *Sphinx*, where, in the wardroom, I was regaled to a splendid meal by those of my brother officers who were not on duty. There was much leg-pulling and many toasts to the future wellbeing of my bride and myself were made. Throughout this ordeal I managed to 'navigate with caution', bearing in mind that later in the day I would need to present some semblance of sobriety.

Not without difficulty, I disengaged myself from my well-wishers and, with the aid of my best man, reached the small Anglican church of All Saints, at Stanley Bay, just in time before the arrival of my bride. On entering the church I was surprised to see the large number of people, both civilian and naval, in attendance. This was, indeed, evidence that the 'steering committee' had been very thorough in their preparations!

After a short wait, Nahidé, looking radiant in a superb wedding gown, with a train held by her two bridesmaids – the young B sisters – entered the church and, to the music of the time-honoured wedding march, walked gracefully down the aisle to join me – to be married for the second time that day!

The service, conducted in English, proceeded smoothly, without any hitches. All rings, when called for, were readily available, and all those present 'held their peace' when the vicar made the usual 'any objections' enquiry to the congregation! Following the register-signing, photograph-taking, confetti showering, kisses and hand-shaking, everyone departed to the nearby B residence, where the reception was to be held.

It was quite late that evening before Nahidé and I were able to board a limousine to take us into Alexandria where, at the famous Cecil Hotel, we had reserved a room for one night. After sampling all the delicacies at the reception, neither of us was hungry enough to face a dinner but, before retiring for the night, we decided to take a liqueur in the hotel bar. Whilst sipping our drinks we were entertained by a *'gilli-gilli'* man (an ambulant native conjuror) who mystified us and the other guests by producing a snake and several tame mice, seemingly from thin air. I remember that his mice were named after famous battles of the Western Desert campaign. Watching the show, I could not help wondering whether the poor mice served the dual purpose of conjuror's assistants and, later, sustenance for the snake!

After breakfast the following morning, Nahidé's two sisters arrived to accompany us to the railway station and give us a send-off. As we lounged in the comfort of the Pullman, Nahidé reminded me that it was almost exactly two years ago that we were on this same train on our way to spend our clandestine Christmas tryst in Cairo. So much had taken place since that memorable vacation. This time we were not travelling as far as Cairo. Our destination was roughly halfway, the town of Tantah, where we were to be met and then escorted to the small village of Dearb Nigm. The reason for this diversion was that, included amongst our wedding gifts, was the generous offer from Leonard and Marianne B to spend as long as we wished at their family farm, which was situated in the heart of the vast cotton-growing area in the Nile Delta region.

Before the marriage, I had been successful in convincing my C.O. that, since graduating from HMS *King Alfred* I had not had any leave, so I was given seven days which, with the kind cooperation of my fellow officers, I was able to extend to ten days, by re-arranging the duty roster. Our plans were to divide the time equally between the farm stay and another visit to Cairo.

Alighting from the train at Tantah, we were given a hearty reception by the farm manager, an affable, elderly gentleman, and his son-in-law, who helped us with our suitcases to their car and then drove us several miles through lush green countryside until we reached the small village of Dearb Nigm. There we pulled up outside a large, imposing, two-storey, European-style villa, on the roof of which was a flagstaff displaying a red flag with a white cross, proclaiming its Swiss ownership. This was to be our abode for the first four days of our honeymoon.

The time passed all too quickly in the pleasant company of our Swiss hosts, who went out of their way to make us comfortable and extremely well-fed (the manager's daughter was an excellent cook). They also spent some time explaining the work involved in the cultivation of cotton in the plantations surrounding the property. The native employees were keen to meet us and regarded me with a certain curiosity, as it so happened that in this remote community I was the first European in uniform they had ever encountered, despite five years of war.

Not only were we both reluctant to abandon the tranquillity of these idyllic surroundings but also the pressure put on us by our hosts to extend our stay was extremely enticing. Nevertheless, we had promised ourselves a return visit to Cairo, knowing full-well that this could be our last opportunity to do so before having to leave Egypt. Also, we had friends there who were waiting to welcome the 'newly-weds', so, early on the fifth day of our vacation, we were driven back to Tantah station to take the train south to Cairo.

We had made arrangements to stay at the Mena House Hotel where, two years earlier, we had been invited to lunch by our friends and, on that occasion, had been very impressed with the 'ambiance' of this famous hotel and its proximity to the most renowned manmade wonders of the ancient world – the Pyramids and the Sphinx.

During our previous stay in Cairo, our programme had been so crammed that we did not find the time to pay a visit to the Khan Khalil native bazaar, which one of our Swiss friends had described as the "true soul of Cairo" and had insisted that a visit there was an experience not to be missed.

After an early breakfast one morning, we ordered a taxi, which took us on a hair-raising ride into the city and then through the congested streets until we reached the bazaar district. Alighting from the taxi, somewhat shakily after our hazardous journey, we found ourselves in a veritable labyrinth of narrow lanes lined with tiny shops, some little more than recesses in the walls of buildings, which appeared to be selling everything under the sun. As we wandered around, our nostrils were assailed by various tantalizing cooking smells, intermingled with the scents of spices, leather, incense, sandalwood and the overpowering perfume of hibiscus.

We passed stalls displaying large piles of nuts of all kinds, dates, fruit and vegetables and others laden with unidentifiable slabs of meat, over which the shopkeepers languidly waved large fans in vain efforts to repel clouds of persistent flies.

Other stores had live rabbits, chickens and pigeons, confined in small coops, all forlornly awaiting their inevitable death sentences.

At every turn we encountered eager store-owners, imploring us to step inside their emporiums and partake of a glass of mint tea, whilst examining their wares.

Some fine silk scarves caught Nahidé's eye and, whilst she was examining these, I entered the neighbouring store, which seemed to specialize in herbal remedies of all kinds. There, on a shelf, was a row of small bottles containing cloudy-looking solutions and bearing labels with Arabic writing, with what appeared to be a coat-of-arms. When I enquired what the bottles contained, I was informed by the storekeeper that it was genuine bath-water from King Farouk's palace – the imbibing of which was absolutely guaranteed to bring me good fortune! I made a speedy exit and rejoined Nahidé!

After a few purchases, all of which involved the habitual lengthy haggling over prices, we made our way back to a taxi-rank, followed by a small crowd of youngsters beseeching *"baksheesh"* in shrill voices.

Within a matter of minutes we were transported back into a totally different world – the Shepheards Hotel – to which we had kindly been invited to lunch by a couple of Nahidé's friends. From time to time, several of my acquaintances had described, in glowing terms, the unique character of this world-renowned hotel but, even so, I was quite unprepared for the opulence with which we were confronted on arrival there.

The public rooms were sumptuously decorated in the Arabesque style. Magnificent carpets, ivory-inlaid furniture, huge sofas and armchairs laden with luxurious cushions, over all of which ornate chandeliers hung from high ceilings. The dining-room service was impeccable and provided by numerous attentive waiters dressed in spotless white *gallibiyas*.

During lunch, our friends told us about the interesting historical background of this hotel. Originally, it had been the palace of a Turkish princess but, in the middle of the nineteenth century it had been acquired and transformed into a hotel by a very enterprising young Englishman, Samuel Shepheard, who saw the need for high-class accommodation to cater to the ever-increasing Victorian tourist trade. He had been a pastry-cook aboard a P&O liner which, when it docked in Alexandria, he had decided to leave to seek his fame and fortune. He had certainly achieved both.

Almost exactly seven years after visiting Shepheards, we were both shocked and saddened to learn of the horrors which occurred there on the day which, subsequently, has become known as *Black Saturday*. In January 1952, a wave of xenophobia swept through the city, when large, unopposed mobs stampeded through the downtown area, looting and burning all European, and especially British, establishments.

One of the principal targets was Shepheards, which the mob forced their way into. They then poured cans of gasoline over all the furnishings we had so admired, and set them on fire. A heroic attempt was made by the city fire brigade to deal with the ensuing blaze but their efforts were thwarted when the overpowering mob slashed their hoses. The flames speedily spread to the upper floors, where guests had taken refuge in their rooms. Many of them, finding themselves trapped, were forced to jump to their deaths from their balconies, much to the delight of the arsonists below.

It was not until late in the evening that the Egyptian army was ordered into the city and a curfew imposed. By that time, a heavy pall of black smoke hung over the city centre – hence the term 'Black Saturday'.

Some time later it was revealed that whilst all this rioting was taking place, King Farouk was holding a reception, following the birth of a son, at the Abdin Palace, less than a mile away from the hotel. It was reported that close aides had whispered news of the disturbances into the king's ear but, apparently, this did not have the effect of interrupting the party!

On the final day of our honeymoon, we were invited to visit a family resident in the garden city of El Ma'adi, located about three miles south of the Cairo outskirts on the east bank of the Nile. There, after lunch, we walked around a beautiful green area, reminiscent of English countryside. In a nearby sports ground, a rugby match was in progress between two Australian army teams, who were being cheered on by a small crowd of mainly military spectators standing around the touchlines.

We stopped to watch. Nahidé was very intrigued, as this was the first time she had witnessed this particular sport and I was busy trying to explain the finer points of the game when a fierce mêlée suddenly took place within just two or three yards from where we were standing.

The sight of a pile of hefty Aussies manhandling each other with blood-curdling yells was too much for her sensibilities and suddenly she cried out, "Tom, do something to stop them!"

The other bystanders were highly amused; I was merely embarrassed!

That evening we had a last meal at Groppi's restaurant and a visit to an open-air cinema before returning to the Mena House.

The following day we said farewell to the famous Sphinx from our bedroom window and, by the late afternoon, I was once again back in HMS *Sphinx* and on duty.

It was my turn for 24 hours on watch as Officer of the Day!

'Here comes the Bride'.

Stanley Bay, Alexandria – indicating All Saints Church.

Floral garland hoisted on the yard-arm at HMS *Sphinx* –
a Royal Navy tradition when one of the ship's company is married.

The happy couple after the ceremony.

Relaxing in the bar at the Cecil Hotel, Alexandria on our wedding night.

Our send-off, by Nahidé's sisters, at Alexandria's railway station.

I Married a Princess

Scenes of activity on the cotton plantation at Dearb Nigm, in the Nile Delta.

The villa at Dearb Nigm, where our honeymoon was spent.

Mena House Hotel, Cairo – taken from summit of the Great Pyramid.

The Khan Khalil Bazaar area of Cairo.

A pastry-maker at work – Khan Khalil bazaar.

19. Surgery and a Sick Cow

We found it hard readjusting to the world of reality after returning from our honeymoon. Fortunately, before leaving I had been able to make arrangements to rent a room in a small private hotel located in the vicinity of HMS *Sphinx*. It had been recommended by Lieutenant George M, who was already staying there with his wife, and her presence provided good company for Nahidé whilst I was absent on duty.

I found a large backlog of work awaiting me at the camp and this involved being on my feet for long hours. After a few days I gradually developed an excruciating pain in the centre of the sole of my right foot – so painful that, finally, I had no alternative but to report to one of the camp's three medical officers, Surgeon Lieutenant Donald F, a dour young Scotsman.

Sitting me in a chair in the Sick Bay, he closely examined my foot and announced, "You've got yourself an ingrowing plantar wart and every time you plonk your foot down you're driving it further inwards, thus causing the pain. It will have to be removed."

Somewhat nervously, I enquired, "How do we tackle that?"

"Oh, it's no problem," he replied affably. "We'll have it out in a jiffy.' With that, he took two bottles out of a cupboard. One contained an antiseptic solution, which he swabbed liberally over my foot. The other bottle contained rum, which he handed to me, saying, "Better take a good swig of that before we start…"

Then, brandishing a razor-sharp scalpel, he dextrously dug out the offending wart. By the time he had finished I was soaked in perspiration brought on, no doubt, by the dual effects of the rum and the actual surgery!

Applying a neat dressing, he then bandaged the foot.

"There you are, laddie!" he announced triumphantly, holding before me, in the palm of his hand, what looked like a small, bloody pyramid.

In a daze, I hobbled out of the room, using just the heel of my foot, and staggered back to the O.O.D.'s office, where I was on duty for the rest of the day.

I sat down with relief, but fully convinced that naval surgery had not changed that much since Nelson's days!

Early in January 1945 we learned, through some friends, of the availability for rent of a small, furnished bungalow, ideally located, facing the sea, on the Corniche road, just a few yards from a sandy, sequestered beach and within easy reach of the naval camp. The rental terms were reasonable and we quickly made the move.

At the rear of the house was a shaded porch, extending the full length of the property, and from this we looked out on an interesting ancient windmill. Beyond this, in the near distance, was a small village, surmounted by its inevitable mosque. Each morning, whilst having our breakfast, we would look out at the slender, lofty minaret, watching the *muezzin* emerge onto a small balcony. There, silhouetted against the rising sun, he would chant his prayers to the faithful residing in the village below.

We were soon feeling quite at home in our new abode. It was idyllic being able to just cross the road for a swim whenever one felt so inclined, and this facility was undoubtedly one of the reasons why we had no shortage of visitors that summer!

We lived well, our victualling requirements taken care of by weekly visits to a small local market, where plenty of fruit, vegetables, eggs and fish were available. One problem, however, was milk, for we had been advised to exercise caution so far as this was concerned and, since moving into the house, we had been using the canned, condensed variety, which after a while had become nauseating.

We were pleased, therefore, when a well-meaning neighbour recommended a milkman who made early morning deliveries of fresh milk. The milkman, an ancient, wizened old gentleman, came around at about-five-thirty each morning. He had a cart, drawn by a donkey which looked almost as old as him, and from one of the large churns in the cart he would fill our *ibrig* (jug). Nahidé would leave this at the front door, together with a small round cotton cover with beads which, when placed over the jug, would guard against the ubiquitous flies.

For a while everything went well, but quite suddenly the smooth routine became unstuck when, for several days, the milk, when heated became lumpy and unpalatable. Nahidé decided to do something about it and I was awakened one morning by the noise of a vehement altercation taking place in Arabic at the front door. I heard the words *"marid katir"* spoken by the milkman several times and hurried to dress so I could join in the action, but before I could, the door was slammed shut.

Nahidé was furious. Apparently, as soon as she expressed concern about the milk's condition, the old fellow had become extremely angry and, instead of being apologetic, had accused us of being very ungrateful people in that his poor cow was *"marid katir"* (very sick) and yet, despite that, was doing her level best to keep us supplied with milk!

That same evening I arrived home with a fresh supply of condensed milk tins…

It was not long after this bizarre incident when, on my birthday in March, Nahidé presented me, not with a present, but with the promise of a future present! She explained that she was expecting our first infant who, according to her calculations, would be putting in an appearance sometime in late October.

I assured her that I was delighted to hear this news, even though I realized that this additional responsibility would complicate matters, bearing in mind that I had no assurance that my present job would continue undisturbed until the war's end. However, with all the optimism of youth, I told Nahidé not to worry and that somehow or other we would overcome any difficulties which the future may throw at us.

We had discovered that, within a short distance to the east of our property, stood the sumptuous summer palace of Montazeh, surrounded by magnificent gardens, and to reach this, King Farouk, always accompanied by a large entourage travelling in several chauffeur-driven limousines, would pass by our house whenever he decided it was time to escape from the searing summer heat of Cairo.

Some years later, in July 1952, it was at this same palace that Farouk received the news that he had been deposed by a group of rebel Egyptian Army officers who, for some time, had been busy plotting a *coup d'état*. He was given just six hours to sign an act of abdication, after which, with all his relatives and many servants, he was escorted under armed guard to Ras-el-Tin harbour in Alexandria, there to board the royal yacht *Mahroussa*, which then set sail for Italy, never to return.

The newlyweds walking on the promenade immediately opposite their bungalow.

This windmill could be seen from the rear porch of our bungalow.

20. A Dog Called 'Salvage'

One day, in early April 1945, I had been visiting an Army friend of mine who was the commanding officer of a unit guarding a POW compound on the outskirts of Alexandria. As I prepared to take leave of my acquaintance, outside the administration building near the main entrance gate of the compound, I happened to glance across the road and noticed a large dog stretched out in the shadow of a shed. I walked over for a closer inspection. A more dishevelled representative of the canine species it would be difficult to imagine. The animal's coat, almost the same beige hue of the sand on which he was sprawled, was matted and filthy and I was about to pass him by when he raised his huge head and glanced directly at me. Instinctively, I murmured, "Hello boy," whereupon his large, expressive eyes lit up and his dense, shaggy tail wagged slowly to and fro, drawing a perfect arc in the sand.

I was hooked. I went back to the office and asked my friend to whom the dog belonged.

"Doesn't seem to belong to anyone," he replied. "He came in the other day with a batch of Jerry prisoners. Maybe his original owner was killed and he just tagged along with the men." He gave me a quizzical glance. "Don't tell me you'd like to have him?"

From the moment that the dog had first looked at me I had been contemplating that possibility. The small seaside bungalow my wife and I had been leasing was somewhat isolated and about two miles east of HMS *Sphinx* and I thought to myself that this formidable-looking creature would probably make a good guard-dog. I hesitated, having no wish to remove him from his rightful owner, if indeed such a person existed, and said as much to my friend.

"For your peace of mind, old man" he said, with a grin, "we'll make enquiries." He walked to his desk, switched on a loud-speaker and, in surprisingly good German, made a brief announcement. Turning to me, he said, "If anyone wishes to claim ownership, he'll have to be here in the next ten minutes."

During the waiting period, I examined the dog, who allowed me to run my hand over him. He was pitifully thin and a worn leather collar hung loosely around his neck, but without any identification. The minutes passed, no one appeared, and Tony handed me a short length of rope with a terse, "He's all yours, chum. What are you going to call him?"

I thought a moment, then replied, "In the circumstances I think that 'Salvage' would be an appropriate name, don't you?"

With the rope passed firmly through his collar, the dog sensed immediately that he was about to go somewhere and pulled himself up on his haunches. I was surprised at his height. I did not know at that time, but later I was to find out that he was a Pyrenean Sheepdog, an ancient breed used by Spanish and Basque shepherds to keep watch over their flocks and guard against attacks by mountain wolves. Except for those occasions which called for ferocity and courage in defending their charges, these dogs were renowned for their very docile disposition.

Without my bidding, Salvage jumped into the passenger seat of my jeep and, glancing sideways at him as I started the motor. I was sure that the despondent expression on his face had changed to one of happy expectancy as we set off on our return journey.

Being off-duty that day, I drove past the camp on the corniche road and straight to our bungalow. By now, I was beginning to wonder what kind of a reception my new acquisition would receive from Nahidé. Any apprehension I had been nursing quickly evaporated, for Nahidé was overcome with compassion at the sight of the dog's neglected state and immediately set to work to improve his lot! On the back porch of the house he was given two bowls – one with water and the other containing a quickly prepared concoction of left-over stew mixed with chunks of bread.

He was obviously famished and, having licked both bowls clean, he stretched out his long frame, yawned, and fell fast asleep.

Later, over a pot of tea with biscuits, I explained to Nahidé the circumstances in which I had acquired Salvage, and, glancing at the sleeping animal, she said, "It must have gone through hell in the desert and probably witnessed many frightful incidents."

Not long after this comment, the sleeping dog shivered and suddenly awakened. It sat up abruptly, with ears pricked, and then, to our surprise, dropped flat to the floor and quickly squirmed across the mosaic tiles to hide under the settee on which we were sitting. Only then did our hearing pick up what his had already done – the distant drone of an aircraft engine – and we realized then that his speedy, reaction was undoubtedly the result of many close encounters with death during his days with the Afrika Korps in the Western Desert.

That evening we tackled the daunting task of washing Salvage. He stood patiently whilst we scrubbed and soaped his large frame but, after we had completed the operation with a final rinse, he showed his appreciation by drenching us both with vigorous nose to tail gyrations!

Whilst washing him we discovered that he was covered with parasitic ticks – the type that get a firm hold with their jaws on their host's skin and then gorge themselves on blood until they resemble small, ripe, purple grapes. To deal with this problem, we devised a de-ticking procedure which thereafter became a routine monthly task. Salvage would jump up onto an old table on the veranda and lie there patiently whilst Nahidé and I, armed with tweezers, would work over his entire body. It was necessary to grip the heads of the ticks as close as possible to the animal's flesh, then tug them out (making sure not to burst the blood-swollen body) and dispose of them in a jar of kerosene. After a while we became quite expert in this exercise!

Within a short time Salvage became one of the family and quietly assumed certain duties without any prompting from us. For example, when we retired at night, he would stretch his full length across the threshold of our bedroom door, remaining there until dawn, giving low warning gruffs whenever he heard any unusual noise in the vicinity of the property.

Frequently, he would accompany me to the naval camp, where he soon became a great favourite of all the personnel, but his size and shaggy appearance intimidated the local native workers, who referred to him as *"Asad"* (Arabic for 'lion').

When taking my turn on 24-hour watch at HMS *Sphinx* one day in five, it was reassuring for me to know that my wife had Salvage as a sentinel during my absence.

Despite the allied victory in Europe in May 1945, the volume of work at *Sphinx* showed no signs of diminishing, as orders came for units of the Mediterranean Fleet to be replenished with fresh crews and made ready for deployment in the Far East. As we listened to reports of the progress of the war there, it seemed grimly obvious that victory was a long way off as the fanatical Japanese fought tenaciously to prevent the allies from setting foot on mainland Japan.

It was in July that we heard "through the grapevine" that, as the work wound down in Alexandria, it was fairly certain that many of the officers and ratings stationed there would be transferred to the Pacific theatre.

Fortunately, however, this was not to be for, for on August 6th and 9th, American B29's dropped atomic bombs on Hiroshima and Nagasaki, with devastating results. Within a month the demoralized Japanese government had surrendered – and we in *Sphinx*, along with thousands of servicemen elsewhere, breathed a collective sigh of relief.

I realized that it would not be long now before I would be receiving my demobilization papers (having, by this time, served for almost six years) and I was informed that I could expect to get these by the year's end.

However, it was not until late February 1946 that the signal arrived with instructions for the Soars family (wife, daughter, and self) to proceed to Port Said, there to take passage on the Cunard liner (now troopship) *Ascania*, due to depart on March 23rd for Liverpool.

Our immediate concern was what to do with our good and faithful Salvage, so "nothing ventured nothing gained" I requested permission to see my C.O. to sound out the possibility of Salvage being added to the Soars list for homeward passage.

Despite my impassioned plea, my appeal was firmly turned down. "The Admiralty is already footing the bill for you and your family. You surely cannot expect to take your menagerie as well," said my C.O., somewhat testily.

We never did forget the reproachful look we received from poor Salvage when the day came to part company and, long after our arrival back in England, we worried about him, wondering how he had fared.

It was not until the winter of 1947 that our guilt qualms were laid to rest. Attending the RNVR officers' Annual Reunion dinner in London I, quite unexpectedly, ran into the fellow-officer in whose hands we had left our dog. Much to my relief, he confirmed that when it came to his turn to leave *Sphinx*, he had been successful in finding a good home for Salvage with a family he knew. What a pity dogs cannot write; imagine the saga he could have related about his war years!

21. A Child is Born

The anglophobic undercurrent in Egypt, which had gradually surfaced once the threat of invasion by the Axis forces had been completely eliminated, became much more pronounced during the summer of 1945. The outlawed Moslem Brotherhood and other extremist nationalist organizations were becoming very active, particularly in Cairo, their aim being to arouse public sentiment against the occupying British forces in any way possible. Leaflets were clandestinely distributed by the propaganda units of these underground movements, urging Egyptians to boycott English-speaking institutions and to cease having business relations with British companies.

One night a large bonfire was set alight in a Cairo street and a mob burnt large quantities of English books and magazines. The ensuing political and social confusion soon spread to other parts of the country, including Alexandria, where gangs, roaming the streets at night, would attack any individuals wearing military or naval uniforms. Stone-throwing, with the targets being military vehicles, became a daily gauntlet to be run and we in HMS *Sphinx* received instructions to have all our lorries fitted with metal grills to protect the windshields. In addition, we took the precaution of adding three armed guards in the back of all lorries.

The nocturnal patrols around the perimeter of the camp were made more frequent and the wire fencing itself was strengthened.

It was at the height of this period of acute tension that our daughter decided that the time had come to enter this world and, after lengthy and painful travail, she, was born at the Italian Hospital on 30th October.

Visiting the hospital, which was located close to the city centre, was a cloak and dagger operation necessitating the donning of civilian clothes rather than my naval uniform and carrying a concealed revolver, just in case of trouble.

A month later, our daughter was baptised in the small chapel in the camp. The ship's bell, turned upside down, was used as a makeshift font by the Chaplain, the Reverend Chetwynd, on what was the first, and probably last, occasion that such a ceremony was performed inside HMS *Sphinx*.

Helene Ingrid Marianne, as she was christened, impressed the large assembly of guests by her perfect composure during the entire proceedings.

The day following this happy event, the news came through from Cairo that Nahas Pasha, ex-Prime Minister and a good friend of Britain, had narrowly escaped an attempt on his life. He was being driven along a crowded thoroughfare when a terrorist had flung a bomb under his limousine but, fortunately for him, the explosion was delayed a few seconds, with the result that a British army lorry, which was following the car, received the full effect of the blast, which seriously injured several soldiers who were passengers.

Worse was to follow. Not long after this incident, a mob set upon and killed, in particularly grisly circumstances, six British soldiers in the main square, opposite the Cecil Hotel, in the centre of Alexandria. What was especially humiliating about this event was the fact that, although repeated telephone calls were made by frantic citizens living in the apartment buildings surrounding the square to the British Army base at Mustapha, in the outskirts of the city, no relief force was sent in to save the men.

The reason, divulged later, was that because of the very delicate political climate, the army command at Mustapha had strict instructions to maintain a low profile and leave the handling of the situation to the local gendarmerie!

As it happened, several suspects were subsequently rounded up and arrested and later an Egyptian judge handed down stiff prison sentences to some of those involved. A few days after this action he was brutally assassinated.

It was astounding that, despite these frightful occurrences, the daily social life in this cosmopolitan city continued, largely unaffected. There were still elegant lunches to be enjoyed at Baudrot's, English teas were still being served in the gardens of the Beau Rivage Hotel, horse-racing, tennis and sailing were regular pursuits. There was no lessening of the numbers of sun-seekers on the beaches of Stanley Bay and Sidi Bishr.

It was as though the Alexandrians were saying, "Sure, we are having problems, but these are nothing compared with what we were facing when the enemy was 'at the gates' during the dark days of 1942."

Proud parents with newborn daughter Helene and naval chaplain, the Revd Chetwynd.

HMS *Sphinx* Church, where Helene was christened.

Proud grandparents with baby Helene.

HRH Salar-ed-Dowleh with his grand-daughter.

I Married a Princess

The Prince in his younger days.

22. Exodus

As the day for our departure from Egypt approached, we busied ourselves with the packing of our meagre collection of personal possessions and, in between, whenever I could seize any spare time from my *Sphinx* duties, we made the rounds to bid farewell to the several relatives and acquaintances we would be leaving behind.

Nahidé, understandably, was facing the leave-taking with mixed feelings, for it was going to be a wrenching experience for her to part company with her parents and siblings. Although the youngest of three sisters, she had been the first to break away from a very close-knit family home. For her parents it was particularly heartbreaking for, so recently, they had been rejoicing in the arrival of their first grandchild, only to have to see it depart for a very distant destination so soon after its birth. They put on a brave face, however, consoling themselves with the thought that their daughter, and her child, were getting away from a country where the present was decidedly unstable and future prospects somewhat dismal.

Since Christmas, several reports had reached us of attacks on allied servicemen by marauding gangs of natives and, judging from shreds of news which filtered through daily, it seemed evident that the day for the official evacuation of all British forces was fast approaching. I was not altogether surprised when, following the usual Sunday morning divisions on the parade-ground, the First Lieutenant asked me to report to his office.

Inviting me to take a seat, he asked, "How goes the packing?"

"Pretty well, sir," I replied, wondering what he had in mind.

"How soon can you be ready to leave here for Port Said?" Before I could reply, he added, "I know that you are not expected to embark on the *Ascania* until March 23rd, but I've been speaking with the Captain and he feels that, bearing in mind your family responsibilities, it would be advisable for you to leave well ahead of that time. The situation here is not going to improve whereas, from all reports, it seems to be a lot calmer in the Canal Zone area." He paused, waiting for my reaction.

"Well," I replied. "Our packing is almost complete, we've said most of our fond farewells, we've found a good home for our dog and, in accordance with your previous instructions, I've parcelled out my duties to the other officers, so I'm sure that we can be ready to leave this week sometime."

He glanced at the wall calendar and said, "Alright then, plan to get away on Wednesday."

Following his gaze, I saw that this day was the thirteenth and replied, "If you have no objection, Sir, I would prefer the following day, the fourteenth, which happens to be my birthday, and may be luckier!"

He smiled and said, "So be it. Fix yourself up with transportation – better take the station-wagon – and I leave all the details to you."

I was about to take my leave when he called me back.

"I don't wish to sound alarmist, but I think it would be prudent for you and the driver of the wagon to carry small arms and also, for extra security, I'll arrange for an armed Royal Marine to come along for the ride."

A thought occurred to me and, thanking him, I said, "I'd like to have Marine W detailed for that assignment, if you have no objection, as he is also a skilled motor mechanic."

No 1 concurred, saying, "Yes, he would be useful to have if you happen to break down in some God-forsaken spot."

I left the office, feeling very appreciative for his obvious concern for the safety and wellbeing of the Soars family.

When I arrived back at the bungalow, Nahidé was visibly jolted when I divulged the news of our earlier-than-planned departure, but she quickly recovered and, immediately after lunch, both of us set to work to complete the remaining packing. We were all ready and waiting when, by dawn's early light on Thursday, the station-wagon arrived to pick us up. Marine W was there, complete with Sten gun, and assured me that he had, the previous day, given the car a thorough examination and had taken the precaution of loading two spare tyres. N, the driver, a burly, good-natured Able Seaman who hailed from Haifa, was equipped with a Smith & Wesson pistol and I carried a similar weapon.

All our worldly goods, baby Helene in her carry-cot and a basket containing provisions for a midday meal for all of us, were soon loaded and, after a last nostalgic glance at the bungalow which had been our home for the last fifteen months, we sped away on our journey.

Port Said, situated almost exactly due east of Alexandria, is only about 140 miles distant as the crow flies, but lying between the two cities is the vast alluvial delta of the Nile which, in those days, had only tortuous meandering minor roads, with many river crossings. After studying the map the previous day, I had decided to keep to the main highways which, although they veered first to the south and then to the north to reach the Suez Canal road that led into Port Said, and thus involved considerably higher mileage, offered, nevertheless, the advantage of being frequently travelled by army and air-force transportation. Also, this itinerary was familiar to me in that I had used it on one or two occasions in the past when visiting certain military camps to barter for needed spare parts for *Sphinx* vehicles.

A possible disadvantage in taking this route was the fact that two or three large towns would be encountered. We passed through the first of these, Damanhur, without any problems, and very soon reached the bridge over the western estuary of the Nile. The next well-populated area was Tanta, where there had been reports of recent spasmodic outbreaks of violence, but, hardly slackening speed, our driver skilfully navigated through the crowded main street and very soon we were clear of the town and heading towards Zifta, where we crossed the eastern estuary of the river.

Now we were in the extensive cotton-growing region and soon reached its marketing centre, Zagazig, where it quickly became obvious, as we headed down the congested main highway, that this was not going to be so smooth sailing as in the previous towns. We had no alternative but to slacken speed as the car became surrounded by a large crowd of chanting natives, who appeared to be taking part in some sort of demonstration. It was decidedly unnerving to have this sea of humans pressing close to the car and peering through the windows and I was not surprised when the clamour awakened the baby who, since leaving Alexandria, had been sleeping peacefully in her cot. Instinctively, my hand tightened around the revolver hidden in my jacket pocket and, at the same time, I cautioned Marine W to have his weapon ready but to keep it out of sight of the mob outside in the street.

The situation was tense, for looking ahead we could see that we were going to have great difficulty penetrating the mass of natives and we realized that it only needed someone to fall under the car's wheels to ignite a very ugly confrontation.

Slowly, we came level with a side-street to our left and, in desperation, I told Able Seaman N to take it – praying that it would not turn out to be a *cul-de-sac*. He pulled over, gingerly, bumping one or two bodies as he did so, but once in the side-street he accelerated to get away from the crowd.

Luck was on our side, for in a matter of minutes the road we had taken wound through a residential district to the outskirts of the town where, opening a road-map, I was able to decipher that we were heading in a north-easterly direction towards the town of Abbasieh, which was on the Canal Road but further north than Ismailia, towards which, had it not been for the enforced change of direction, we would have headed.

Shortly afterwards we arrived, without further incident, on the west bank of the Canal, where we located a pleasant shaded area overlooking the water. Nahidé unloaded the luncheon basket, the contents of which soon disappeared. The long journey, plus the excitement of the recent close encounter had whetted our appetites! Whilst eating, it was interesting to watch the different types of shipping passing us, only a short distance away, especially as, from our perspective, one got the impression that the vessels were actually gliding over the sand.

After the meal we resumed our journey, quickly covering the remaining thirty miles to Port Said where, at Navy House, I reported to the O.O.D., who confirmed that he had received a signal from *Sphinx* and was therefore expecting our arrival. He seemed relieved when I mentioned that we had accommodation arranged with friends ashore for, no doubt, he had been wondering what kind of billet he could locate for a married couple with one small child.

I left his office and we then drove over to Port Fouad, a relatively new residential garden city on the Asian bank of the Canal where, at the home of close friends of Nahidé's family, we received a warm welcome. When being advised of our plans for sailing from Port Said, they had, most generously, offered us a place to stay until such time as we could board the ship.

Soon, our small mountain of baggage was unloaded and we bade farewell to Able Seaman N and Marine W, for whom I had arranged with the O.O.D. at Navy House for overnight accommodation in the naval barracks. After the incident during our journey, I was worried about their safety during the return trip and, late the following day I telephoned through to *Sphinx* and was relieved to learn that they had reported back 'on board' after an apparently trouble-free return journey.

Our hosts, a young married couple, made us feel very much at home during our short stay and, after we had settled in, were keen to show us around the immediate area. We gladly accepted their offer, knowing full well that this could be the last opportunity in our lifetime to explore this historic waterway and its environs.

We were taken to see the famous impressive bronze statue of Ferdinand de Lesseps, the Frenchman whose insight, determination and energy enabled him to realize his life's dream – to connect the Red Sea to the Mediterranean. The figure, on top of the high pedestal, faces eastwards, with hand outstretched towards the canal entrance, welcoming, as it were, ships to his achievement.

We were also fortunate enough to get special permission to view the town and harbour from the dizzy height of the magnificent lighthouse which, somewhat incongruously, is located in the business section, with banks, shipping companies, consulates and offices as close neighbours.

Time spent in pleasant company and interesting pursuits passes quickly and, in the afternoon of March 23rd, our hosts drove us down to the passenger ship quay, where we found the Cunard liner *Ascania*, which had arrived the previous day. It had travelled from India and en route had made several ports of call to pick up UK-bound passengers who, for the most part, were married service personnel with their families.

Visions of having a cosy cabin to ourselves quickly evaporated, for to obtain the maximum use out of the space available, the ship's peacetime cabins had all been refitted to accommodate, in spartan fashion, as many as four – and in the larger cabins six – adults. Families were split up, with women and children separated from husbands, and Nahidé, with Helene, finished up in a crowded four-bunk cabin with three other women and two other small infants. I was directed to an even smaller cabin on another deck, which I shared with three officers, of junior rank like myself.

Not a particularly memorable commencement to what I had been hoping would be a comfortable homeward-bound trip but, as we strolled on deck later that evening, watching the shore lights of Port Said recede into the distance, Nahidé and I consoled ourselves with the thought that the duration of the voyage would probably only be about ten days.

As it happened, an improvement in the sleeping arrangements was achieved the following day when, after an almost sleepless night for the occupants of Nahidé's cabin, I made an impassioned appeal to the ship's Medical Officer, who arranged for Nahidé and Helene to be transferred to the ship's sick bay (which was empty). This benefited not only them, but also improved the space situation for those remaining in the cabin.

No sooner had we made the transfer than the alarm sounded, summoning all passengers to boat drill stations. This was to be a daily routine, for although the Med had been considered sufficiently safe for troopships and merchantmen to sail between Port Said and Gibraltar unescorted since early in 1945, there still existed the possibility of encountering a floating mine, despite the herculean efforts of our minesweeping flotillas since the cessation of hostilities.

When the exercise was over, Nahidé and I were taking a stroll around the deck to work up an appetite for lunch when, suddenly, a voice behind us said, "Tom Soars, isn't it?" I turned to see a neatly-attired RAF officer, arm-in-arm with a pleasant-looking woman in Nursing Sister's uniform. It was Frederick P, a chum from my schooldays, who I had not seen since before the war, and he introduced to us the Nursing Sister, Margaret, whom he had married quite recently. We also became acquainted with another couple, Lieutenant RNVR Alan J and his wife Denise, and during the remainder of the voyage the six of us, plus Helene, who was the centre of adulation, spent many a happy hour together.

As we progressed westwards at a steady fourteen knots, just out of sight of the North African coast, it was difficult to realize that we were so peacefully traversing the dangerous corridor which, for over three war years, had become known to allied shipping as "bomb alley". To the south of us were towns, the names of which had become famous during the ebb and flow of the ferocious Western Desert campaigns – El Alamein, Mersa Matruh, Sidi Barrani, Sollum, Bardia, Tobruk, Derna, Benghazi, Tripoli and so many others came to mind.

On the fourth day we entered the Straits of Sicily, passing, to the south of us, the gaunt, pyramid-shaped Italian island of Pantellaria and we realized, to our disappointment, that the ship had already passed by Malta.

There had been much speculation on board that we were to call at Malta en route and my friends and I had been hoping to have the chance to revisit this island fortress which, in recognition of the tremendous resistance its population had shown through so many months of almost daily enemy aerial bombardment, had been awarded the George Cross.

We consoled ourselves with the thought that now it was almost certain that Gibraltar would be our first port of call, where, hopefully, we would get the opportunity to spend a few hours ashore.

However, this was not to be! Three days later having sighted, in the late evening, the small Spanish island of Alboran, with its lighthouse, we calculated that we were approximately one hundred and thirty miles due east of Gibraltar and so we retired, feeling sure that during the night we would be arriving at the Rock.

Awakening early the next morning, I was surprised to find that the ship was still under way and, dressing quickly, I rushed up on deck to find that we were well out at sea. Both to port and to starboard I could distinguish shore lights, but these appeared to be gradually receding into the distance. I knew then that we were already passing through the Strait, having left Gibraltar behind, and that the lights I could see were probably those of Tangier in Morocco and Tarifa on the Spanish mainland. Later, at breakfast, this was confirmed by one of the ship's officers, who also told me that our final destination, Liverpool, would be our only stop on this voyage. A pity that we were not made aware of this from the outset; it would have spared us a lot of speculation!

After breakfast we passed Cape Trafalgar, off which Nelson's great victory took place and, as we headed into Atlantic waters, the weather remained very fair, even crossing the Bay of Biscay, notorious for bad seas, it continued to be quite calm.

Within a day or two we were in home waters and, early in the morning of April 5th, we made a point of going on deck so that Nahidé could get her first ever glimpse of Blighty, but unfortunately, as the ship entered the Mersey estuary, visibility was poor, due to a heavy, low-lying mist. Slowly, we approached the docks and finally came alongside a quay, adjacent to the Cunard Building. As we did, so the mist lifted and the early morning sun revealed a very familiar landmark – the gilded bird perched high on top of the Royal Liver Building.

Our friends joined us on deck as gang-planks were being lowered and, together, we watched the hive of activity on the quayside below. Numerous officials and baggage handlers started to swarm aboard and our attention was drawn to a group of camera-carrying individuals who were making a determined advance through the crowd towards a gangway.

"That lot seem to be newspaper reporters," said my friend. "There must be a V.I.P. on board."

About thirty minutes later we discovered who was their quarry; it was the Soars ménage!

23. Oh to be in England!

To ensure an organized disembarkation, groups of passengers were being called by name to be ready to leave the ship so, having completed our packing, we remained on the upper deck, taking in all the activity on the dockside below. Completely absorbed in this operation, we were taken completely by surprise when suddenly, a voice behind us said, "Lieutenant Soars, please excuse us."

I turned around to recognise the same group of men who we had seen previously on the quay and realized, all too late, that we had been cornered by the press. Guardedly, we answered a few questions, whilst the cameras got into action but, fortunately for us, the interview came to an abrupt end when one of the ship's officers, with excellent timing, came up to tell us that we were supposed to be in the group now being disembarked.

Nahidé, with Helene in her arms, scampered off immediately, only too pleased to escape this unexpected ordeal, but before I followed I paused to question one of the reporters as to how he was aware that we would be arriving on this particular vessel. All I got in reply was the usual stereotyped response, "Sorry, Sir, but we cannot reveal our sources of information!"

In the taxi, on the way to the Lime Street Station, I did my best to placate Nahidé over this unwanted publicity and the two of us racked our brains as to who, amongst our many acquaintances, could have divulged the information regarding our homecoming.

We were still trying to fathom this out when we drew up to the station entrance, where we became preoccupied unloading and transporting our luggage, preparatory to boarding the London train. It was not due to leave for a half hour and, whilst waiting, I telephoned, as prearranged, our friends in Sandgate, near Folkestone, who had offered us temporary accommodation on first arrival.

Finally, we boarded the train, which appeared to be crowded, but fortunately the naval travel warrant with which I had been issued covered first-class seating and we found that we were able to spread ourselves out in a carriage all to ourselves. Both of us, and the baby, even managed to get a short sleep, which compensated for our waking up in the very early hours of the morning.

It was with some apprehension that we alighted from the train at Euston Station for, after the encounter in Liverpool, we fully expected to be confronted by more gentlemen of the press but, to our considerable relief, none were around.

We found a very obliging porter, who quickly loaded our baggage and found us a taxi.

For Nahidé, the drive across the city which, up to then, she had only read about, was enthralling. En route, I pointed out sites of interest, including Nelson's column in Trafalgar Square, where our driver stopped briefly and where Helene was delighted to see the ubiquitous flights of pigeons.

We found that we had over an hour to wait at Charing Cross Station before the departure of the Folkestone train and, having had only coffee and biscuits since leaving the ship, we were feeling famished. Not wanting to go to the trouble of lugging the baby's carry-cot and all our belongings into a restaurant, we opted for a lunch *al fresco* and found an unoccupied bench, where I left the family whilst I made a foray in search of something to eat.

Fifteen minutes later I returned, triumphantly bearing the traditional English meal of fish and chips, wrapped in the daily newspaper! The aroma was appetising and we tucked in with gusto.

Nahidé, all the time, was taking a close interest in the hustle and bustle of the busy station. Several years later I was to recall this particular incident when, during one of my many visits to the Public Records Office at Kew, I was able to unearth an old government document entitled "The visit of H.M. the Shah of Persia to Great Britain". It described, *inter alia*, the arrival at 5 p.m. on 18th June 1873 of a special train at Charing Cross Station from Dover. On board was a very important personage – none other than the Shah Nasr-ed-Din, the first Persian ruler ever to visit Great Britain.

A large excited crowd packed the specially decorated station and, on the platform where the gaily-bedecked train came to a standstill, stood a resplendent guard of honour as well as a host of dignitaries. After a few minutes, the Shah emerged from the royal compartment, descended to the red carpet where their Royal Highnesses The Prince of Wales, Prince Christian and the Duke of Cambridge awaited to greet him on behalf of Her Majesty Queen Victoria. After the usual cordialities, the Shah, followed by his retinue of forty-six persons, accompanied the three Princes to the Queen's carriage, which was waiting in the station forecourt. Then, escorted by a detachment of the Royal Horse Guards, the carriage, at the head of a lengthy cortege, clattered through the crowd-lined streets to Buckingham Palace, where the royal visitor was to be the guest of Her Majesty for several days.

Now, almost seventy-three years later, that Shah's great grand-daughter had arrived at the same railway station, but in somewhat different circumstances!

"Sic eunt fata hominum"!

The Soars family, during our first days back in England,
Folkestone Promenade, April 1946.

The *Daily Express* report and photo taken on our arrival in Liverpool.

24. If You Know the Right People…

Throughout the war years, I had maintained contact with both the management and my former colleagues at the Insurance company where I had been employed before joining the navy and when, early in 1946, I mentioned in correspondence that I was soon to be demobilized, I was delighted to receive a reply from the company offering me a job upon my return to England. This took a considerable weight off my shoulders, bearing in mind my recently-acquired family responsibilities.

The company had a small service office in Maidstone, Kent and it was agreed that I would take up my duties there as a Junior Inspector by the first of May. So, after two weeks with our friends in Sandgate, we once again packed up all our belongings and moved to Maidstone, where the Company had found temporary accommodation for us in a rather genteel guesthouse on the London Road, within close walking distance of the office.

The day after settling into our new abode, I travelled up to London to undergo my demobilization routine, which included receiving a farewell gift from the government consisting of a complete set of ready-to-wear "civvies", dressed in which, and feeling rather self-conscious, I arrived 'home' in Maidstone. Nahidé, accustomed to seeing me in uniform, was taken aback, whilst little Helene was scared of the "stranger" who had suddenly appeared in her young life!

Whilst staying in Sandgate we had spent some time with our friends, delving into the intricacies of life in post-war Britain, and this included mastering the complications of the ration book system. After our time in Egypt, a land of plenty, we found the food shortage aspect difficult to get used to. Not surprisingly, a black market existed, but to participate in this we were given to understand that it was necessary "to know the right people". It was not until after almost two years that I became involved in an incident which actually confirmed this axiom.

After a visit to the Company's Head Office in London, I was making my way to London Bridge Station to take the train back to Maidstone when I could not help noticing, coming towards me, a young fellow dressed in a somewhat garish, purplish-blue, double-breasted suit with white stripes and wide lapels, and sporting a multicoloured tie. To my surprise, as he drew level, he looked at me closely, stopped, and said, "Hello, Sir." As I turned in my tracks he added, "Remember me, Sir? I'm Able Seaman X."

Then, I recognised the face, under the brim of the trilby hat, as a young Cypriot seaman who had been one of the naval transport drivers under my command at HMS *Sphinx* and, as I shook his hand, I recalled the occasion when, a few days prior to my leaving Alexandria, he had come to see me for permission to go before the Captain as a requestman. Like quite a number of the personnel in *Sphinx* he had been enlisted locally, but now that he was approaching the end of his "hostilities-only" service, he was sounding out the possibility of being demobilized in the United Kingdom, so that he could join members of his family who were resident in London. He had provided me with evidence of this and, as he had been an excellent rating, I had no hesitation in passing on his request to the C.O., supported by my recommendation.

That was the last I had heard about it. Apparently, it had subsequently been approved and, eventually, he had been discharged in a home port. He seemed to be overjoyed to have bumped into me so unexpectedly and pleaded with me

I Married a Princess ~ 167

to come and meet his family. It was still early for my train, so I agreed to do so, and he hailed a taxi, giving the driver an address in the West End. It transpired that the address was his uncle's restaurant, where, on arrival, it was explained who I was. I was then given a tumultuous reception by all the members of his grateful family, who were insistent that I remain for a meal with them. Faced with such friendliness, I could not refuse the invitation.

The meal was superb – easily the best I had eaten since returning from overseas – and when it was all over and we were chatting and sipping Turkish coffee, my erstwhile naval driver disappeared, with his uncle, into the kitchen. After a while they reappeared, the uncle holding a football-size brown-paper parcel which he handed to me, saying, "Please take to the missus as she is not here to eat with us."

I thanked him for his generosity and, after much handshaking and well-wishing, a taxi was called to take me to the station, at which I arrived just in time for the train back to Maidstone.

I found a corner seat in a carriage with four other passengers and, after carefully arranging my briefcase, hat, raincoat and the paper parcel on the luggage rack above me, I sank back into my seat and opened my evening newspaper.

It was warm in the compartment and soon I was beginning to feel drowsy. Suddenly there was the sound of a subdued splash and, simultaneously, there appeared on the page of the newspaper I was holding, a red blotch which, to my amazement, gradually soaked into the newsprint.

Furtively, I cast a glance at my fellow passengers, all of whom, to my relief, seemed quite oblivious to this bizarre occurrence, but as I looked upward I saw, to my horror, that blood was oozing through the brown-paper package. Even as I looked, a second drop fell and plopped on to my cheek. Quickly, I pulled out my handkerchief to mop my face, hoping that it looked as though I was having a nose-bleed, but, by this time, two of the other passengers had noticed the incident and were regarding the parcel with a certain interest.

With magnificent nonchalance, I rose to my feet and adroitly turned the parcel over and, at the same time, placed my folded-up newspaper beneath it. I then sat down, opened my briefcase and, as though nothing had happened, pretended to show a concentrated interest in certain files.

There was an ominous silence and I could almost feel the enquiring glances being cast in my direction and at the mysterious parcel on the rack, but typical English reticence prevailed and not a word was spoken.

I spent the remaining twenty minutes before arriving at my destination praying fervently that the newspaper would absorb any further seepage and, at the same time, nursing an uneasy feeling that my fellow passengers would be leaving the train absolutely convinced that they had been sharing a compartment with some kind of a serial killer who was, no doubt, on this way to dispose of a decapitated head!

Arriving home, I presented Nahidé with the parcel, which she opened to reveal a sight for sore eyes – a most handsome sirloin of beef, surrounded by several strings of pork sausages!

This made all the discomfort of the train journey seem well worthwhile.

25. Impulse Buying

It was a splendid mid-June morning. The sky a clear blue with just a vestige of cloud and the air warm with a light breeze as I boarded the Chatham-bound bus at the Maidstone depot. My plans for the day were to introduce myself to the Company's agents located in the Chatham-Rochester-Gillingham triangle and, the promised Company car not yet being available, public transportation plus *Shanks's pony* were my only means of travel. Little did I realize, as I took my seat on the upper deck of the bus, that before me waited quite an eventful day.

I was absorbed in what had become almost a daily routine – scanning the properties for sale columns in the local newspaper – when, suddenly, an advertisement caught my eye. It read:

> "Desirable detached brick residence, freehold, situate in two acres off scenic Blue Bell Hill, midway Maidstone and Chatham. Price £1,250. Apply 'Berwyn', Kingswood Road, Kits Coty."

This certainly seemed too good to be true and obviously the situation called for rapid action as, judging from the description of the location, the property could be somewhere along this bus route. Grabbing my briefcase, I clattered down the stairs to the bus conductor standing below and, brandishing my newspaper, asked him if he knew the whereabouts of Kingswood Road.

"It's a good job you asked me 'ere chum," he replied, "as it's the next stop you want. We're now on Blue Bell Hill and that house would be somewhere down there." He waved vaguely into the dense woodland on the side of the highway and, seconds later, he rang the bell to bring the green double-decker to a shuddering halt on the steep gradient.

Thanking my informant, I jumped off and stood at the side of the road, feeling somewhat out of place in these almost wilderness surroundings, dressed as I was in my new navy blue business suit, with black homburg, and carrying my shining new briefcase. My erstwhile fellow passengers must have had similar thoughts, for several faces regarded me through the windows with ill-concealed curiosity! The bus lurched away to continue its slow, uphill climb and gradually the sound of its motor receded into the distance, leaving me in complete silence, broken only by the occasional twittering in the nearby thicket.

I strode a few yards back down the hill to where, from the bus, I had noticed an opening in the thick woods and there found, half hidden by creeping vine, a dilapidated, weatherworn sign, bearing two words – *Kingswood Road*!

I set off down the deeply-rutted lane, thankful that it was a dry day and, after walking for about half a mile, the woods on the left-hand side of the track gave way to a large clearing, occupied by a small white bungalow, surrounded by various farm buildings.

Beyond these buildings I could see ploughed fields with, in the distance, a splendid view of the Medway valley with a village (which later I was to discover was Aylesford) straddling the river.

Pausing by the gate leading to the house, I could see several chickens and, in the rear meadow, some cows, but no sign whatever of human presence until, quite unexpectedly, a face materialized from behind a high screen of runner beans and a voice with a pronounced Kentish accent enquired whether I wanted to buy fresh eggs. The owner of the voice, a slightly-built, wiry individual, wearing a flat cap, worn overalls and rubber boots, then approached the gate.

Producing my newspaper, I pointed out the advertisement, which only thirty minutes before I had circled on the bus, and asked if he could direct me to the property.

"You wouldn't be thinking of buying it?" he questioned, as he removed his cap to reveal a bald pate, which he then proceeded to mop with a grubby handkerchief.

"It's possible," said I, politely, but at the same time thinking to myself that it was obvious, surely, that I would not be down is this remote location, with a newspaper if I merely intended to have a picnic!

"Well, that's "Berwyn", he said, pointing down the lane in the opposite direction from which I had just come. About a quarter of a mile away I could make out the top part of a yellow brick house, standing on an eminence, with an impressive backdrop of dense forest rising high above it. I thanked him for his assistance and continued on down the lane, drinking in the idyllic vista of sharply rising woodland on my right and, to my left, a panorama of meadows and ploughed fields stretching far into the distance.

Approaching the house, I could see that it stood at the very end of the lane – beyond it there was nothing but trees. Passing through an open and ruined gateway, I stood at the top of a sloping path that led down to an untidy garden, in the middle of which, surrounded by several foraging hens, was a woman busily engaged in hanging washing on a line.

I called out, "May I come down? It's about the advertisement in today's paper."

The woman removed a peg from her mouth and remarked, "I saw you in the distance, talking to Mr White, and I thought you might be selling something."

A reasonable enough assumption, I considered, in the light of my attire and briefcase.

"No, I'm interested in buying the house and I take it you're the owner?"

"Wish I was," laughed the woman. "Me and me husband are just tenants and we're moving away, as he's been transferred. I suppose you'd like to have a look around. The owner told me that he was advertising the house but I didn't expect anybody so soon."

I helped in propping up the laden clothes-line and spent the next half-hour examining the property, both inside and out, with the woman providing a running commentary.

The house was unquestionably of superior construction and had been well maintained. The rooms on the ground floor were spacious and handsomely finished with wood panelling and hardwood floors, whilst upstairs the three bedrooms and bathroom were reasonably decorated. In fact, as I explored the premises I found myself wondering why a house of this quality should have been located in such an isolated location. The same house, in a suburban setting, would have a price-tag of from two to three times the asking price which appeared in the newspaper.

The very remoteness would not appeal to many would-be purchasers, but to a young family, living out of suitcases in a cramped bed-sitting room in a guest house located on one of the busiest streets in Maidstone, it seemed to be an answer to a prayer. To be sure, it had little to offer in the way of "mod cons" – no electricity or telephone, but lighting was available from a large metal container of calor gas and, in all the rooms, including the bedrooms, were fireplaces. A huge black monster of a range in the kitchen was, according to my guide, "ideal for cooking and baking" and the water supply was excellent. The main intake pipe descended almost vertically from a storage tank at the top of the hill behind the house and, when the household taps were turned on, the resultant pressure was reminiscent of a fire hose in action!

The tour of inspection completed, I advised the woman that I was very interested in acquiring the property and she wrote the owner's name, address and telephone number on the back of an envelope. I thanked her for all her ready assistance in showing me the house and was preparing to depart the way I had come when she announced that there was a 'quick way' up to the main road. She indicated a footpath at the edge of the woods at the rear of the premises and, once again thanking her, I plunged into the forest.

During the next fifteen minutes I found myself scaling a precariously steep incline, the likes of which I imagined that even Tarzan would have preferred to avoid! Eventually, dishevelled, scratched and perspiring, I burst forth from the thick undergrowth and found myself near the top of the hill on the main Chatham-Maidstone highway.

I managed to reach the bus-stop just in time to flag down a Chatham-bound bus and gratefully staggered on board. Glancing at my watch I discovered that the entire operation, since first observing the newspaper advertisement, had taken less than two hours and that I would arrive at my destination in good time to keep the few appointments I had arranged.

Before lunch, I telephoned the owner, who lived in Maidstone, and arranged a meeting for the following day. Within less than four weeks all the legal formalities had been completed and the Soars family had become the proud owners of what was, in our opinion, one of the most attractive pieces of real estate in the 'Garden of England'.

Considering that only a little more than two months had elapsed since we had disembarked at Liverpool, this was no mean accomplishment!

'Berwyn' – our first house, on Bluebell Hill, Near Maidstone, Kent.

A cold first winter in the UK for Nahidé and daughter Helene.

26. Moving In

For the day of our removal we were fortunate enough to have Dame Fortune smile upon us. The weather was perfect, friends with cars readily rallied to our aid and the Maidstone firm which had been storing our three crates of household possessions had kindly consented to delivering, without extra cost, on a Saturday morning. The driver of the removal van had some very uncomplimentary remarks to make regarding the condition of the track leading from the main road to the house but, apart from this, the entire operation went very smoothly. We had an alfresco lunch, after which our friends departed.

As the noise of their departure receded into the distance we suddenly felt very much alone. We were. There was not a soul to be seen in whichever direction we gazed from our vantage point on the step of the front door, which faced south towards the distant Medway valley. Tearing ourselves away, with difficulty, from this idyllic interlude, we entered the house to continue the task of unpacking and arranging the small amount of furniture we had been able to acquire since our arrival back in England.

Busily occupied with all the chores indoors, the time passed quickly and, before we knew it, the sun was beginning to descend below the brow of the hill behind the house.

Leaving Nahidé to make some soup and sandwiches, I decided to make .a more detailed examination of the grounds around the property and, leaving the kitchen door, I strode towards the edge of the forest, where I found a rudimentary wire fence which, evidently, marked the property line. Following this fence I was able to gauge an idea of the actual perimeter of the property and the size of the plot, which seemed even larger than the two acres referred to in the title deeds.

My meandering took me to the southern edge of the land, where there stood a fair-sized wooden structure, the sides and roof of which were covered with heavy black tar-paper. I remembered seeing this shed from a distance during my first visit to the house and because on that occasion it was surrounded by chickens, I assumed it was a chicken-house. I was about to retrace my steps when I heard a faint noise within the shed, so I opened the door and peered inside. To my astonishment I found that the gloomy interior was full of chickens. Most of them were huddled together on perches, others on the floor, but all of them seemed too weak to move and, in reaction to my sudden entry, were able only to emit a few nervous squawks. On the floorboards, covered with a thick layer of accumulated droppings, were several dead birds.

It was obvious that these poor birds had been locked in the shed when the previous occupiers of the house had packed up and left which, judging from the condition of one bird I picked up, must have been two or three days ago. I dashed back up to the storage adjacent to the house and found a shovel and a bucket. Filling the bucket with water I returned to the chicken-house and filled the completely dry trough on the floor. I was somewhat relieved to find that six of the hens, presumably hardier than their sisters, had emerged and were making desultory attempts to find some food in the grass around the shed. Lifting the others one by one off the perches, I carried them outside, noticing as I did so, that their breastbones were as sharp as razor blades. They did not have sufficient strength to move around to forage and could only squat where I had placed them.

Some kind of grain was essential immediately if I was to carry out a successful relief operation, but I could find absolutely nothing left behind in the storage shed.

On informing Nahidé of the predicament, she had one of her brainwaves.

"We'll give them rice," she said, in a matter-of-fact tone, and promptly disappeared into the larder. (Here, I should explain that, having been forewarned by various relatives and friends of the severe post-war shortage of certain commodities, we had made a point of packing in our crates some of these – including two pillowcases full of rice.)

When I scattered the precious grains near the crouching birds, most of them, to my delight, devoured it ravenously but, unfortunately, some were too far gone to make the effort to eat.

It was already dark by the time I had removed all the dead birds and buried them in a common grave. I had also shovelled out the layers of dirt from the floorboards of the shed and, recollecting vaguely that I had read somewhere that this made good manure, I had put it into a neat pile. Most of the hens re-entered their house voluntarily, but I had to carry one or two of the more feeble birds inside and place them on a perch. That task finally completed, I closed the door and found my way back up the hill to the kitchen, where Nahidé was busy putting the baby to sleep in her cot. The small breakfast room adjoining the kitchen was to serve as her bedroom once everything was settled but, for this first night, she was to remain in the warmth of the kitchen.

I poured myself a cup of coffee and sat at the kitchen table, relaxing in the warm glow of the range, but soon I started to itch around my collar and down the front of my shirt, so much so that my scratching was soon observed by Nahidé. She cane over to the table to investigate and her sudden high-pitched squeal startled me.

"You are crawling with lice!" she exclaimed.

I took a close look down at my chest and it was very obvious that I was having an acute attack of *pediculosis* – in other words, I was lousy! Evidently, during my erstwhile rescue operations a large percentage of the hens' lice population had transferred itself onto my person. I was speechless, but Nahidé's reaction was swift and dramatic. I was ushered out of the back door and ordered to strip down completely. I stood there, shivering in the cool of the evening, until Nahidé' appeared with a pail of water, into which she had poured a bottle of vinegar. This concoction was sponged all over me from head to toe and then I stood there, feeling very miserable, whilst Nahidé fetched a second instalment of water, this time accompanied by a bar of carbolic soap. These ablutions terminated, I was subjected to a close inspection by torchlight, after which I was pronounced free to associate once more with fellow humans and allowed back into the house, to a most welcome change of clothing!

Before falling asleep that night, my thoughts scurried over the events of the day and as Nahidé jumped into bed I said, "Well, that's something I couldn't have done in a house in the suburbs."

"What's that?" enquired Nahidé, drowsily. "Stand stark naked out in the back yard."

With that, I fell fast asleep.

27. Easy Come, Easy Go

Having discovered an ancient but still serviceable scythe amongst the piles of vintage utensils in the tool-shed, I was, that Saturday morning, attacking the veritable jungle of long grass and weeds that had been allowed to grow unchecked all around the house.

Although not yet ten o'clock, the August sun was extremely warm and when Whitey hove into view at the top of the driveway I was more than glad of the opportunity to take a breather. We passed the time of day and Whitey, surveying the extent of the grass, commented, "What you need here are three or four geese."

"What I really need around here," I replied, "is a motorized lawnmower."

"Geese are better than lawnmowers," replied Whitey, with authority. "What is more, they can live on grass. They eat as much as sheep and need but little extra food, except for an occasional basin of mash, mixed with kitchen scraps." Warming to his theme, he added, "They don't need any housing, they're first-class sentinels and what's more, goose eggs make for good eating."

I was convinced. The following Wednesday, it being the day of the weekly farmers' market in Maidstone, I set off, after an early breakfast. The car was laden with sixteen chickens, packed in four crates. These birds, all Rhode Island Reds, I had selected from the twenty-two survivors of the original starving flock which I had stumbled upon that evening of the previous month when we had moved into "Berwyn". I had figured that all we really needed for our household requirements were six good laying hens and, with the money to be obtained from selling the surplus, I could probably afford to purchase the desired quota of geese.

After some bouts of haggling with one or two local townsmen, I succeeded in disposing of my chickens for five pounds. Then, the serious business of scouting around for some young geese started. Eventually, I came across three most handsome grey birds, sitting docilely in a large crate on the tail-board of a lorry, the apparent owner of which was leaning against the vehicle, quietly picking his nose in a state of deep meditation. Cautiously interrupting his train of thought, I enquired, "Are these your geese?"

"Them's mine," he replied.

"For sale?" I asked.

"Could be," he said.

"How much do you want for them?"

Pursing his lips, and after studying his feet for some time, he replied, "Two pounds ten shillings each."

That would get me just two birds, I thought, fingering the five recently-acquired pound notes nestling in my trouser pocket, but Whitey had recommended that at least three geese should be obtained.

"How much if I take all three?"

The goose-owner went into deep thought and, finally, after a deep sigh, said, "I'll let them go for six pounds the lot."

That seemed a most reasonable price for three birds that seemed to be prime examples of their species.

"That's with the crate included, I hope?"

"Yes," he replied. "And that's a real bargain you've got there, sir."

I handed him the precious pound notes I had received in exchange for my chickens, plus an extra pound from my wallet.

With the help of its late owner I manoeuvred the heavy crate into the boot of my car and, with a sense of satisfaction for a job well done, I set off for home. I drove slowly, out of respect for my passengers but they, finding themselves suddenly mobile, set up a strident chorus, which startled the shoppers all the way up the crowded high street.

Whitey was working in his garden when I arrived back, so I stopped the car to show off my recent acquisitions. Peering closely at the geese through the slats of the crate, he expressed his approval and readily agreed to accompany me to Berwyn to assist in off-loading my precious cargo.

As I brought the car to a standstill, close to the back door of the house, Nahidé, holding Helene in her arms, came out to watch, whilst Whitey and I manhandled the crate out of the boot. During this stage of the operation, the three new arrivals were strangely silent, no doubt adjusting to their new surroundings. Filled with pride of ownership, I untied the cord which held the lid of the crate, raised it carefully, and stood back to admire these three fine new additions to the Soars ménage.

The geese craned their necks high to look around and then, one by one, scrambled clumsily out of their confinement and, cackling in unison, waddled a few yards, under our admiring gazes.

Then, to our combined astonishment and dismay, the three birds suddenly took to the air with a violent thrashing of wings and, within a matter of seconds, were circling well out of reach over our heads!

As we watched, absolutely speechless, the three birds made a preliminary reconnoitring flight around the house and then, in line ahead, set a course in the direction of Chatham, disappearing forever over the brow of the hill to the rear of our property.

It was only then that my mentor Whitey said, "Why didn't you make sure at the market that their flight feathers had been clipped?"

Thus it was, in my first venture into livestock husbandry, that I learned the hard way!

28. Summer's Lease

In the pre-war years, as a member of one of the rowing crews of the Brighton Cruising Club, I had participated in annual regattas, hosted by the coastal towns of Dover, Deal and Folkestone, but these were hectic one-day outings and, as such, did not offer any opportunity to really become acquainted with the county of Kent. So I was extremely happy with my appointment as a Junior Inspector attached to the Company's Maidstone Office, as this was to give me the opportunity to discover the county's hinterland.

Maidstone (pronounced "Medstun" by the natives) was the county town, beautifully situated, straddling the meandering River Medway and boasting many fine old Tudor buildings, some dating from the fourteenth century.

May was a wonderful time of year to arrive in this town, for the vast apple and cherry orchards in the surrounding countryside provided breathtaking vistas of white and pink blossoms which, framed in the springtime greenery of adjacent woodlands and hop fields, offered sights not easily forgotten. Frequently, beneath the fruit trees, could be seen flocks of sheep with their long-legged newborn lambs, forming perfect pictures of pastoral peace.

Our new abode, being located in such scenic surroundings, and yet within easy reach of London, attracted many visitors that first summer. Old friends, from our naval days, and those newly acquired since arriving back in Blighty, as well as relatives, came for day visits and for weekends, always being careful to bring with them comestibles to supplement our meagre food rations and, taking full advantage of the perfect weather, we had many a splendid picnic outdoors. After the bleak war years it was paradise to lie out in the sun after a satisfying meal and listen to the chorus of songbirds from the nearby woods and the distant lowing of cattle from the fields below the house.

There were also the occasional unexpected, and uninvited, visitors. About three miles, as the crow flies, to the north of our property was the village of Borstal, close to which was the institute of the same name, which housed young offenders. From time to time, youngsters would manage to escape and could cover a lot of ground by travelling through the thick woodland before breaking through to the open fields close to our house, then fleeing downhill towards the village of Aylesford, sometimes with guards in close pursuit.

On one occasion, during my absence at work, Nahidé was hanging washing on the clothes-line in the back garden when one of these escapees actually burst out of the woods right into our field.

With remarkable *presence d'esprit* she turned towards the house and yelled at the top of her voice, "Tom, there's a Borstal boy here, get your gun!" To her relief, this ploy had the desired effect, for he bounded off like a deer and rapidly disappeared down the hillside. It was at times like this when we thought of our dear dog Salvage and realized how much we missed him.

On another occasion, when I arrived home one evening, Nahidé casually announced that she had had a visitor. "A very nice old fellow called Moore," she said, "and he sold me this." She pointed to a copy of *Old Moore's Almanac* lying on the dining-room table!

In July a letter arrived from the Admiralty, which contained the official confirmation of my release from service, but with the added caution, "Maintain one uniform in good condition in case of the need for recall." I had given no thought to this possibility and the sudden reminder of such an eventuality cast a temporary shadow over our happy, carefree summer.

I did comply implicitly with this, my last naval order, and my No.1 doeskin uniform, complete with mothballs, was carefully packed away in a trunk.

Fortunately, I was never recalled, but my uniform was… Many years later, when we were living in Montreal, the son of a good friend of ours was to be married. He was in the naval reserve and, for the ceremony, was facing the expense of a new uniform. He was exactly the same build as I had been in 1944 and my suit fitted him perfectly – all it needed was the rank insignia changed and several days of airing to eliminate the mothball odour!

Thus, on the day of the wedding, I had the unusual experience of seeing the suit I was married in walk down the aisle for a second time!

29. The Winter of our Discontent

Gradually, the time-honoured tints of a beautiful mellow autumn succeeded the unusually warm summer of 1946 and, still revelling in the delights of our newly-acquired home, we were well and truly lulled into a state of false security.

Had we had an inkling that the approaching winter was to become notorious as one of the most severe on record, especially in the south-east corner of England, there is no doubt that we would have had sober second thoughts on the wisdom of having located in such an isolated rural retreat.

It was not until the last week in October that a sudden drop in temperature, accompanied by heavy rains, prompted me to lay in extra provisions. Also, to take care of our heating and cooking needs, I purchased another Calor gas container. This was stored away in the shed where, very soon, it became surrounded by piles of logs and kindling wood – the end products of several evenings and weekends of backbreaking sawing and chopping.

Our "black monster" range in the kitchen had already demonstrated an insatiable hunger for combustible materials and the firewood stocked in the shed was to supplement the very meagre ration of household coal allowed in those difficult post-war years. In addition to the range, there were open fireplaces in the other rooms of the house which, in the absence of any form of central heating, would have to be used if it became too cold.

At the end of October, my travelling to and from the Company's office in Maidstone and around the province was made easier when the long-promised car, a Triumph Mayflower, finally arrived. No longer would I have to face the wearisome bus and train journeys in order to maintain contact with the Company's agents throughout my large area.

However, this most welcome improvement in my mode of travel was to be of short duration!

Early in December we awakened to find the house extremely cold and unusually silent and, opening the curtains, we were amazed to see a white mantle stretching to the horizon. Winter had arrived with a vengeance!

After breakfast, it was only with considerable difficulty that I was able to navigate my new car along the narrow rutted track between the property and the main highway, which was about a mile distant. As winter progressed, bringing further heavy snowfalls, the track became impassable so that, finally, I had no option but to park the car at the end of each day in an open clearing just off the main road and then trudge from there to the house.

Looking back on the vicissitudes of that winter, I marvel that we managed to adapt to conditions so completely different from our years in the Middle East and, happily, both my wife and myself survived without developing any serious ailments.

The cold weather intensified and, by the beginning of January, we were forced to abandon our upstairs bedroom when we discovered that the water in a tumbler by our bed had frozen. Thereafter, we slept in the living-room, where there was a much larger fireplace in which we maintained a permanent fire. We had already placed Helene's cot in the small breakfast room which, adjoining the kitchen, benefited from the warmth of the range, which we kept stoked with a mixture of coal and small hardwood logs.

The main disadvantage to our revised sleeping arrangement was that with the one and only bathroom being on the upper floor, it required our donning headgear, scarves and topcoats whenever it became necessary to answer the call of nature!

As the wintry conditions worsened, we heard over the radio, urgent appeals for the services of experienced skiers to deliver essential basic provisions to some of the more remote villages which had become completely isolated due to the blizzards.

One evening, I decided to re-locate from the poultry-house to the shed close to the house, our six remaining Rhode Island hens (the survivors of the ill-fated flock we had inherited on the day we moved into the property). I first installed a small oil-stove in the shed to provide a modicum of warmth for their well-being.

It was late in the evening as I staggered through the snow-banks with the last pair of complaining hens, one tucked under each arm, that I noticed, in the fading light, something resembling a small fur glove lying close to the wall of the house, and, after depositing the two hens in their new abode, I returned quickly to investigate the object. I found, to my surprise, that it was a tabby kitten, it's small body inert and, judging from the fur which was raised in hard spikes, apparently frozen to death. I tucked the creature inside my jacket and took it into the kitchen for closer inspection. Nahidé took the stiff body from me and, pressing her fingers into the pitifully small chest, announced excitedly that it was still, alive.

We wrapped Lazarus (as he later came to be called) in an old pullover, which we placed carefully in the hearth in front of the living-room fireplace and, miraculously, after a few minutes, his limbs shivered and his eyes opened. We went into the kitchen to prepare some warm milk, but almost immediately we heard a noise from the other room. Returning to the room, I found that a small burning log had rolled off the grate and had taken up position beside the cat. The pullover was already afire and there was a smell of singed fur as the weakened animal struggled to escape.

Quickly, I unfurled the cat from the burning pullover and within a short time it was contentedly lapping up the milk from a saucer, apparently none the worse for its ordeal through ice and fire!

Lazarus soon gained strength and soon made himself at home in his new surroundings, but we did not realize that his stay with us was destined to be of short duration.

About two weeks after this incident, Helene, now just fourteen months old, developed a running nose and a troublesome cough and her breathing became strained and noisy. Her temperature registered well above normal and, obviously, medical attention was needed.

To have taken her to a doctor in that condition was out of the question and, in any case, I could not have carried her from the house to the main highway, so I had to find a doctor who would come to the house. I plodded through the snow to our neighbour's house and used his telephone to call the closest physician, who happened to reside in Aylesford, the small village about two miles away, which we could see, in the distance, from our house. The doctor was at home and I explained the situation to him. To my relief he said that he would come the following morning and I started to advise him of the necessity to leave his car just off the main road when he said, "I won't come by car". Before I could ask further questions he abruptly put the phone down, leaving me wondering what means of transport he had in mind.

Helene had a restless night and, after breakfast the following day, we anxiously awaited the doctor's arrival. Looking through the sitting-room window, Nahidé drew my attention to a slowly-moving black dot in the far distance in the direction of Aylesford. Gradually, the dot became larger and then we could make out the figure of a man carrying a bag but, oddly, instead of trudging through the snow, he appeared to be gliding over the surface.

Thirty minutes later, the doctor was in our kitchen, unlacing an ungainly pair of snowshoes from his boots, explaining as he did so, that a relative from Canada had made him a present of these before the war!

Turning to us after his auscultation, he said, "she has croup, an infection of the larynx and trachea, quite common in small children. She must be kept very warm and her chest and back rubbed with camphorated oil. And if I was you," he added, "I'd get rid of *that*." He pointed an accusing finger at Lazarus, who was contentedly purring away in his box near the stove.

"Why?" I enquired.

"Has the baby been in contact with other children or have either of you had colds or the flu recently?" he enquired.

I replied in the negative.

"Then," summed up the doctor, "it is an allergy, which she has picked up from the cat."

Later that week, Lazarus was introduced to Whitey, our neighbour, who was only too pleased to have another cat to add to his anti-mice squad, which patrolled his various farm outbuildings. Both of us were sorry to have to part with him after so short an acquaintance, but we persuaded ourselves that it was for the best.

We learned, several years later, that Lazarus had lived to a ripe old age, during the course of which he had added a considerable number of offspring to the local feline colony!

30. Farewell to 'Berwyn'

Slowly, very slowly, winter's grip on the land loosened, but it was not until the end of March before I could risk bringing the car from its improvised parking place near the main road back to our house. The enforced loss of use of the vehicle had caused me considerable inconvenience, particularly in late February when our stock of coal, despite careful husbandry, had become sadly depleted. From my office in Maidstone I telephoned the coal merchants to order the balance of our winter ration to be delivered, but when it failed to materialize the following day, as had been promised, I phoned to enquire the reason why.

The person I contacted explained that the driver, having surveyed the state of the track to the house, decided that it would have been unwise to risk making the delivery. In the light of my own experience I was not altogether surprised to hear this, but I had been hoping that someone, with a heavier vehicle, could have been more venturesome. Sensing my disappointment, the voice on the phone said, "What if we dump the bags at the end of the track just off the main road? Could you handle them from there?"

I had no option, so I reluctantly agreed to this arrangement. Also, I felt certain that Whitey, our neighbour, would be prepared to assist with the aid of his tractor.

That evening, as I turned in off the main road, twelve sacks of coal greeted my arrival. I parked the car and trudged along the track to Whitey's bungalow, only to discover, to my chagrin, that he was in bed with a bad bout of influenza. His wife offered me the use of the tractor, but I declined, on the grounds that I would probably have wrecked the machine, and myself, at the same time.

Coal being a scarce commodity, I could not leave it there, so, after returning home for a change of clothing, I tackled the task of manhandling the bags, each weighing about fifty pounds, myself. Even though I was in relatively good physical condition after six years of naval life, I was forced to spread the job over two days. It took about two weeks of daily massaging with embrocation to ease the excruciating pain in my back and arm muscles!

When the spring-like weather returned, it became routine to put Helene in her pram in the garden on the south side of the house for her mid-morning siesta. One morning, Nahidé went out to bring the pram in to give Helene her lunch and, just as she entered the kitchen, there was a most alarming sound and the room became momentarily darkened as an avalanche of melted snow fell past the window from the roof.

Hurrying outside to inspect the damage, we were astonished to find long, jagged shards of broken cast-iron guttering protruding from the huge mound of snow now occupying exactly the same spot where the pram had been, just moments before. We shuddered as we considered the consequences had Helene been left outside just a little longer.

It was this occurrence which, strangely enough, was instrumental in our uncovering the history of the property. The following Monday I made enquiries in Maidstone to find a firm to repair the damage, and was recommended to Building Contractors called Hughes & Son. After describing our disaster to Graham Hughes, I was surprised to learn that he knew exactly where our isolated abode was located.

"That property was built by my uncle in the early thirties," he explained.

"But why," I enquired, "did he choose such a remote location?"

"Actually, he didn't," replied Graham. "It was his girlfriend. It was like this. They were engaged and he had promised his bride-to-be that he would build her a house wherever she decided she would like to live. One day, it happened that they were having a picnic on the top of Bluebell Hill and, from that vantage point, she pointed down to the foot of the hill, where the forest meets the open country, and announced that that was where she wanted her house to be built. Soon they were married and, true to his promise, "Berwyn"(Bernard was my uncle's name and Wyn his wife's) was duly constructed."

The guttering was speedily and efficiently repaired and, as a result of this chance encounter, we became firm friends with Graham and his wife, a friendship which was to endure well over fifty years.

Whilst we welcomed the arrival of spring, we really had no choice but to face the reality of *non semper erit aestas* and seriously consider moving to more urban surroundings. So, after considerable soul-searching, we decided, by mid-April, to put the property up for sale. The very first prospective purchaser, a retired gentleman from the north of England who was planning to start a chicken farm, thought that the house, with its surrounding field, was ideal for his purpose and a price agreeable to both parties was duly arrived at. The arrangement was, however, subject to his obtaining financial assistance from his bank.

Two or three days later, on a Saturday morning in the middle of a torrential rainfall, a dapper gentleman wearing a bowler hat and carrying a briefcase and umbrella, presented himself at the house. He introduced himself as the local bank manager and was in a vile temper. Because of the glutinous condition of our track he had, wisely, left his car near the highway but he had completely underestimated the hazardous nature of the walk to the house. Halfway along, he had slipped and fallen on his back and was now copiously plastered in mud from the collar down to his spats.

Fearful that this contretemps could prejudice his attitude to the required loan, we plied him with liberal quantities of tea and sympathy!

It must have helped, for we later learned that the purchaser had got his loan and that the property was to change hands on June 15th.

Gradually we packed, but as the weather became warmer with the promise of perhaps another balmy summer, we began to suffer misgivings. However, the die was cast, and we now had to concentrate our efforts towards finding alternative accommodation closer to civilization.

Our neighbour, Whitey and his wife, who had been so helpful to us during the 'dark days', were sorry to learn of our impending departure, but we assured them that we were only going as far as Maidstone and would drop by to visit them from time to time.

"Make sure you do," said Whitey, then added, "there'll always be some fresh eggs when you come."

The removal day went off without a hitch. The van driver had little trouble navigating down the now-dry track to the house and the removal men quickly packed the small amount of furniture we had been able to acquire since our return from overseas. After the van left, we finished loading the car with our remaining personal baggage and then carried out a last check inside the house, including one long nostalgic glance at the black monstrosity of a kitchen range which had kept us alive during that hard winter.

Returning to the car, Nahidé took the paper bag she had been mysteriously keeping aside and, with it, then walked completely around the house, pouring salt from the bag as she did so.

Noticing my quizzical look when she returned to the car, she said, in a matter-of-fact voice, "that should keep all the evil spirits from following us – just an old Middle East custom!"

As I drove down the highway to Maidstone, I reflected that it was almost twelve months since we had moved into 'Berwyn' – a year that had been a most unusual melange of happiness and misery.

There was a copy of *Picture Post* magazine lying on a table in our room when we checked into the Royal Star Hotel that after-noon. On the front cover was a picture of Easter chicks and the caption underneath read, 'The Easter symbol of hope after Europe's worst winter since the Middle Ages'.

"And don't we know it," I murmured to myself.

31. A Small World

"*Ma'aleechm*," muttered my lunch table companion, when the waitress advised him that the steak and kidney pie he had just ordered was "off". Hearing this familiar Arabic expression indicating "it doesn't matter" I was immediately intrigued.

It happened to be my day to visit Canterbury and environs and, having left Maidstone early that morning, I had, en route, already called on the Company's agents in both Faversham and Sittingbourne. Arriving in the cathedral city at around midday, I had decided to have lunch before embarking on further calls. I had located a restaurant, which had an interesting menu displayed in the window, and went inside, only to find that, already, all the tables were occupied and a small queue was being organised by an efficient young woman, brandishing a menu.

Advancing down the line, she was asking if anyone was willing to share a table and I readily volunteered. I was then ushered to a small table in the centre of the dining-room, where the young fellow already sitting there indicated that he had no objection to my joining him. Thus it was that I was sitting opposite him when I overheard the familiar phrase.

Being advised that his preferred meal was no longer available, he settled for sausages and mashed potatoes and I ordered the same. Studying the man opposite, I could see that he was about the same age as myself and was wearing an RAF tie. By way of opening a conversation I said, "I gather that you must have spent some time in the Middle East."

He gave a pleasant grin and replied, "Isn't it amazing how these bits of Arabic stay with you?"

"How long were you out there?" I enquired.

"Oh, off and on, I suppose about four years, mainly at the base in Dekheila in Egypt. Were you RAF?"

I mentioned that I had served in the Navy and towards the end of the war had spent most of my time in Alexandria.

"Oh, Alex," he said. "That's where I got married.

"That's interesting," I replied. "I was also married in Alex."

He was on the point of continuing when the arrival of two orders of 'bangers and mash', with all the accompaniments, brought the conversation to a halt and several minutes passed while we both tackled the food before us. Then the RAF-type said, "I married a Wren from the naval base; I suppose you also married a service girl?"

Swallowing my last mouthful of sausage, I explained that I had married a civilian whose family was residing in Alexandria, not far from Stanley Bay.

"As a matter of fact, it was at the small English church. I believe it was called 'All Saints' in Stanley Bay where I got married."

"What an extraordinary coincidence! That's the same church *we* were married in," exclaimed my table companion.

During dessert our conversation drifted into the recounting of wartime experiences and mutual problems now being faced by both of us on "civvie street", but over coffee and a cigarette the RAF-type mused, "How strange that we two should bump into each other here," and then, after a pause, "as a matter of interest, what year were you married?"

"44," said I, "in December."

"December 44," he repeated. "Tell me, exactly what date?"

"On the second," I replied.

"Good Lord!" he said, his voice raised to a pitch, which I noticed was causing patrons at the other tables nearby to regard us in somewhat pained surprise, "But that was our day too!"

When he said this, a vision of the churchyard flashed through my mind and, once again, I saw the carpet of confetti on the flagstones as I had entered the church that December afternoon and, to the surprise of my companion, I said, "then your wedding must have been around 2pm on that day. Ours was about two hours later."

"Bang on!" he replied, and then added, "then I suppose it is to you that my bride and myself owe the splendid array of flowers which were already in the church when we entered?"

This was quite true, as some good Swiss friends of my wife, whose homes were nearby, had decorated the church that very morning with flowers in abundance from their extensive gardens.

We finished our coffee, paid our bills and, feeling somewhat lightheaded from the excitement of this extraordinary encounter – the odds of which must have been several million to one – we made our way to the city car-park where, yet another coincidence, our cars were parked almost next to each other. There we exchanged addresses and phone numbers and were just about to part company when my new-found friend said, "Here, hang on a minute, didn't you say that you had a youngster?" With this, he opened his car and dragged out a very large black leather case which, when opened, revealed many small glass jars containing baby food. "I didn't tell you that I'm a traveller for Heinz. Here, take these home as a memento of our brief encounter!" He placed about a dozen jars in a paper bag, handed them to me, and, after shaking hands, we went our separate ways.

We never did see each other again. Not long after that incident my company transferred me from Maidstone to

Brighton and, fully occupied with a new job in different surroundings I somehow did not find the time or opportunity to communicate and, no doubt, the situation was identical so far as he was concerned.

Epilogue

It seems but a short while ago that the events recalled in this book took place but *tempus fugit* and, as one ages, the faster time appears to fugit!

On the second day of December 2006 we celebrated sixty-two years of marriage, thus firmly refuting the gloom and doom predictions of some of our more sceptical wartime acquaintances that such a union couldn't last.

I suppose that sixty years plus in wedlock can be regarded as quite an achievement in this 'brave new world' when marriages of short duration (if indeed they take place at all) seem to have become the norm.

Following a somewhat nomadic existence, during which the exigencies of my career took us to different parts of the world, we spent our retirement years settled in Ontario, Canada.

Here we live in relatively contented obscurity having, in the words of the 'Desiderata': *"taken kindly the counsel of the years, gracefully surrendering the things of youth."*